DAILY PRAYER MINUTES

for

TEEN GIRLS

DAILY
PRAYER
MINUTES
for
TEEN
GIRLS

365 Comforting

Conversations with God

BARBOUR
PUBLISHING

Print ISBN 978-1-63609-773-2

Cover Design: Greg Jackson, Thinkpen Design

Published by Barbour Publishing, Inc., 1810 Barbour Drive, Uhrichsville, Ohio 44683, www.barbourbooks.com

Our mission is to inspire the world with the life-changing message of the Bible.

Member of the
Evangelical Christian
Publishers Association

Printed in China.

Day 1
YOUR PLAN
FOR MY LIFE

God, I spend a lot of time thinking about the future and wondering what my adult life will look like. Right now I go to school, I spend time with my friends and family, and extracurricular and church activities take up the rest of my time. But I wonder what will happen when I'm done with school—what will my life look like then? The Bible says that You have a plan for each of us. Help me to trust Your will and Your plan for my life. Thank You for the future that You have in store for me. Amen.

For you created my inmost being;
you knit me together in my mother's womb.
Psalm 139:13 NIV

Day 2
STAYING IN BED

Lord, some days I just want to stay in bed and pull the covers over my head. I don't want to be with people because people can be mean and hurtful and scary. All I really want is to be loved and accepted. And the more I think about it, I guess that's what everybody wants. Help me love others the way I want to be loved. Help me to make the people I encounter feel good about themselves. I want to be the kind of person who makes people want to get out of bed. . .not stay under the covers and hide. Amen.

"My command is this: Love each other as I have loved you."
JOHN 15:12 NIV

Day 3
A FOREVER HOME

God, heaven sounds like an awesome place. I've heard about it a lot. I know that people don't just go in the ground; they live somewhere else *forever*. Help me remember that eternity is more important than this world. I don't know how long my life here on earth will last, but eternity never ends. It will be totally wonderful to spend forever with You in heaven! I want my friends and family to be there with me too, God. Help me tell them about You so they can be ready to meet You someday. Thank You for my eternal home in heaven. I love You. Amen.

"There is more than enough room in my Father's home. If this were not so, would I have told you that I am going to prepare a place for you? When everything is ready, I will come and get you, so that you will always be with me where I am."

JOHN 14:2-3 NLT

Day 4

PLANS FOR
TOMORROW

Lord, there are so many things on my mind, it's often hard to fall asleep. One thing I do know is that no matter where I am or what I am doing, You are watching over me. Thank You for blessing my life, for making sure I have everything I need. Thank You for guiding me when I am not sure what I should do. Thank You for protecting me. Tonight, I will close my eyes, trusting that You will keep me safe while I sleep and that I will wake up to a new day of fresh possibilities with You by my side.

The Lord is my Shepherd [to feed, guide,
and shield me], I shall not lack.
PSALM 23:1 AMPC

Day 5
THE BEAUTY
OF THE HEART

Heavenly Father, I want to be a young woman who honors You in every aspect of my life, including the choices I make regarding how I dress and present myself. Help me be aware as I continue to mature that the clothes I wear and the amount of makeup on my face send a message to those around me. I ask You to give me confidence in who I am as Your daughter. Help me believe that I am beautiful just as You made me and that I don't need to add a lot of "extras" to my appearance.

Your beauty should not come from outward adornment, such as elaborate hairstyles and the wearing of gold jewelry or fine clothes. Rather, it should be that of your inner self, the unfading beauty of a gentle and quiet spirit, which is of great worth in God's sight.

1 PETER 3:3–4 NIV

Day 6
NOWHERE TO RUN

God, Psalm 139 says that You know everything I have done, am doing, and will do. Nothing is hidden from You. You go before me, leading me every step of my life. I feel like the psalmist when he says, "Such knowledge is too wonderful for me, too great for me to understand!" (Psalm 139:6 NLT). Even if I tried, I couldn't get away from You! You would run right after me. There is nowhere I can go to get away from Your presence. Ever. A love like Yours is impossible for me to grasp. But I am so thankful. Amen.

O LORD, you have examined my heart and know
everything about me. You know when I sit down or stand
up. You know my thoughts even when I'm far away.
PSALM 139:1–2 NLT

Day 7
A GOOD MODEL

Father, Your Word tells me to guard my heart (Proverbs 4:23) and that Your peace will protect my heart as I follow Jesus (Philippians 4:7). Thank You for those wise words of wisdom!

The Bible is Your Word to us, and I believe it is alive and active (Hebrews 4:12). Your Word is the bottom line—the source of truth. Please let the role models in my life live by it and always point me toward the truth. Help me to remember that anytime I'm confused by what someone says about You, I can turn to Your Word for the truth. Amen.

Join together in following my example, brothers
and sisters, and just as you have us as a model,
keep your eyes on those who live as we do.
PHILIPPIANS 3:17 NIV

Day 8
THOUGHTS

Lord, help me keep a positive attitude. Help me to think of good things. Plant Your Word in me so that I will keep in mind all the things You say are important—loving others (even enemies), obeying my parents, being kind to everyone, forgiving people (including myself), taking care of my body, and being content in every situation. Help me to make Your Word my word in all I do and say. Build me up within to look on the bright side no matter what is happening on the outside. Each day give me a new heart and mind focused on Your light. Amen.

For as he thinks in his heart, so is he.
PROVERBS 23:7 NKJV

Day 9

YOUR INSTRUCTION BOOK

Sometimes I wish I had an instruction manual for my life, Lord, but then I realize You've already taken care of that. You've given us Your Word to guide us through this journey on earth. I can read about how much You love me, how You forgive me, and what I need to do to act and live wisely. Thank You for not expecting me to try to figure things out on my own. You have given me Your Word so that I can grow closer to You. Thank You for sharing Your "instruction manual" with me! Amen.

All Scripture is inspired by God and is useful to teach us what is true and to make us realize what is wrong in our lives. It corrects us when we are wrong and teaches us to do what is right.

2 TIMOTHY 3:16 NLT

Day 10
FORGIVING MYSELF

Dear God, I get so frustrated with myself sometimes when I mess up and don't do things perfectly. When I see how far I really am from perfect, it sometimes makes me feel hopeless, like there's no point in even trying to be good. When I start thinking this way, help me to remember that You didn't create me to be perfect and that what I do has no influence over how much You love me. There is nothing I could do to make You love me more, and nothing I do could make You love me less . . .and I thank You for that gift. Amen.

If you kept record of our sins, no one could last long.
But you forgive us, and so we will worship you.
PSALM 130:3–4 CEV

Day 11
THE GIFT OF FRIENDSHIP

Dear God, thank You for the friends You have given me. I am so thankful for each one, and I ask that You would continue to bless all my friendships. Help me remember to put others first and to settle any disagreements with kindness and gentleness. Show me how to serve my friends, whether it's listening to them vent when they've had a really bad day or surprising them with their favorite candy. I want to be a good friend and show them how much I care. Thank You for being the perfect example of a friend who loves at all times. Amen.

But the wisdom from above is first of all pure. It is also peace loving, gentle at all times, and willing to yield to others. It is full of mercy and the fruit of good deeds. It shows no favoritism and is always sincere.
JAMES 3:17 NLT

Day 12

CONTROLLING
MY ANGER

Lord, I read in Your Word that You were angry once—in the temple, when people were turning Your meeting place into a store of sorts. What was meant to be a holy place was instead filled with those trying to make some money. I get angry when I feel used too! But I can learn from Your example. You were angry but didn't let it lead to sin. You dealt with the problem and moved on. I know I shouldn't let my anger get out of control. Please help me to keep it in check so that it doesn't develop into hostility.

Understand this, my dear brothers and sisters: You must all be quick to listen, slow to speak, and slow to get angry. Human anger does not produce the righteousness God desires.
JAMES 1:19–20 NLT

Day 13
SAVED BY A GIFT

Father, thank You for the plan of salvation. The Bible says that everyone living on earth is a sinner; we are all far from You. But You didn't want us to be lost forever, so You sent Your Son to pay for our sins. Thank You for the cross—for making a way for me to be in a personal relationship with You. Thank You for taking my guilt upon Yourself and giving me a clean heart. I have friends who don't know about Your good news, Lord. Help me to be a light shining for You. I want to tell others about this great gift. Amen.

For the wages of sin is death, but the gift of God
is eternal life in Christ Jesus our Lord.
ROMANS 6:23 NKJV

Day 14
A WAY OUT

Lord, I face a ton of temptations every day. It could get really aggravating if I didn't know a few things. First, I'm not alone. Lots of people are tempted. And You, God, have promised to help me be strong—and You will show me a way out! I don't need to feel trapped but just look for whatever exit You've provided. Best of all is the fact that if I do cave, You will not only forgive me but help me be stronger the next time. So, thank You, Lord, for being greater than any temptation I will ever face. Amen.

The temptations in your life are no different from what others experience. And God is faithful. He will not allow the temptation to be more than you can stand. When you are tempted, he will show you a way out so that you can endure.
1 CORINTHIANS 10:13 NLT

Day 15

BEING CONTENT WITH ORDINARY

I wish I could be content with being "average," God, but it's hard when culture says you shouldn't be. I guess I should be encouraged when I think about all the average people I've read about in the Bible. Many of them were just ordinary people doing ordinary things, and yet You used them. David was a shepherd boy. . . Mary was a small-town girl. . . But You knew their names, and You had a plan for them. Help me remember that You have a plan for me as well. Amen.

"For I know the plans I have for you," declares the LORD, "plans to prosper you and not to harm you, plans to give you hope and a future."
JEREMIAH 29:11 NIV

Day 16
JUST BEIN' ME

Lord, everywhere I look there is someone with "more" than what I have. Please help me to see the positive, to enjoy the ordinary and appreciate what I do have, and to not complain about what I don't have in my life. Jealousy and envy cannot change my circumstances but will only make me bitter. If I am focusing on others instead of You, my view becomes blurred. I want to see myself through Your eyes. Please help me to live differently than the world around me. Teach me to recognize all You have given me, and help me to become all You created me to be. Amen.

Let us not become conceited, or provoke one another, or be jealous of one another.
GALATIANS 5:26 NLT

Day 17

THOSE WHO WAIT

Forgive me for my impatience, Lord. I struggle with waiting. I confess, the same is true when I come to You in prayer. I make a request and wonder if You've even heard me when I don't receive an answer right away. And sometimes I think You've forgotten me or stopped listening to my prayers altogether. But I know that isn't true. Please help me as I wait. Remind me that faith sees before it receives. You are faithful in Your promises to me through Your Word. I know I can pray in faith and You will answer. Amen.

We do not want you to become lazy, but to imitate those who through faith and patience inherit what has been promised.

HEBREWS 6:12 NIV

LIVING THE FAITH

Lord, there are a lot of people who don't really care about others' feelings. They've said things about me and my friends that hurt! Help me remember that they probably don't know anything about You and that deep inside, they are longing for the love that only You can give. Open doors for me to share Your love with them, even if I don't feel like it at the time. Help me be a good friend and point them to You. Show me how to live out my faith in You, Lord. Amen.

"Do to others whatever you would like them to do to you. This is the essence of all that is taught in the law and the prophets."

MATTHEW 7:12 NLT

Day 19
IS ANYONE LISTENING TO ME?

You are a loving God who considers each of His children precious. No one is so far away that You cannot hear them. You not only hear my loud cries, You hear my softest whisper and even know the feelings inside my heart that I can't form into words to speak. Help me to remember in those moments when I cry, *No one understands me or even hears me!* that You *always* hear me and You care. There is nowhere I can go that You do not see or hear me. I can have the assurance that no matter what happens to me, I will always have a friend who thinks I'm worth listening to. Amen.

"You are the God who sees me."
GENESIS 16:13 NIV

Day 20
SHE'S NOT LIKE US

God, please forgive me for judging others! Help me to remember that "different" doesn't mean someone is "less" than me. And please remind me every day that Your Word says we are supposed to be different from the world—set apart, holy. Fitting in isn't the most important thing. . .being like You is! So, when I see people who are different from me, let me see them through Your eyes, Father! You're not looking at the clothes they're wearing or the way they're wearing their hair. You are only looking deep inside at their hearts. Amen.

"The LORD does not look at the things people
look at. People look at the outward appearance,
but the LORD looks at the heart."
1 SAMUEL 16:7 NIV

Day 21
A SERVANT'S HEART

Lord, as someone who believes in You and what You teach, I am called to a life of serving others and putting them before myself. But because we were all created differently, You have given us different ways of serving one another. Help me to use the gifts and abilities that You have given me in a unique way to serve those around me. I may have gifts that I'm not even aware of! Open my heart to what You would have me do, make my heart sensitive to the needs of others, and give me creative ways to show Your love. Amen.

The Spirit has given each of us a special way of serving others.
1 CORINTHIANS 12:7 CEV

Day 22
LOTS TO LEARN

Dear Father, thank You for teachers. Yes, I know sometimes I complain about the homework they assign and the tests they give, but I want to say thank You anyway. Forgive me for the times I've been disrespectful in my attitude and words about my teachers. Help me keep my mouth shut and walk away when others begin to do that. Thank You that I live in a country where education is available to everyone. Thank You for the teachers who get up every morning, come to class, answer my questions, and grade my papers. Help me show them that I appreciate them. In Christ's name, amen.

Listen to advice and accept discipline, and at the end you will be counted among the wise.
PROVERBS 19:20 NIV

Day 23
GIVE ME COURAGE, PLEASE

Heavenly Father, I've read about people of courage in the Bible; there was David and Ruth and Daniel and Esther and Mary and Paul and so many more. Lord, these people had confidence in You and knew that You would give them the strength they needed. I need that kind of courage and confidence too. Please work in me so I can live for You and bring You glory. I don't want to be weak and cowardly and ashamed of You and Your Word. I want to be bold in my witness for You; I want to live courageously. I ask this in Your name. Amen.

"Be strong and of good courage, do not fear nor be afraid of them; for the Lord your God, He is the One who goes with you. He will not leave you nor forsake you."
DEUTERONOMY 31:6 NKJV

Day 24
GOD'S DELIGHT

You are with me. You are a mighty Savior. You take great delight in me. You will calm me with Your love. You even rejoice over me with singing! I am so happy to know that You delight in me! You look down from heaven, and You smile because You created me and Jesus wiped my sins clean. I don't have to worry that You're angry with me or disappointed. Jesus paid for my sins once and for all (1 Peter 3:18), and I can rejoice in knowing that You see me as a beautiful daughter. Amen.

"For the LORD your God is living among you.
He is a mighty savior. He will take delight in you
with gladness. With his love, he will calm all your
fears. He will rejoice over you with joyful songs."
ZEPHANIAH 3:17 NLT

Day 25
I BELIEVE!

Faith seems like such a simple concept, Father, but it's sometimes the hardest thing to do—believe in something that I can't see. It's not only about the faith that You exist—I take You at Your word, even though I cannot prove it. I believe everything in Your Word is true and that I should live my life obeying it, because that's the only way I will have true success. Some people will fail me, Lord, and will cause me to lose faith in them; but You have promised that You will never fail me. I can rest in complete confidence that You will always love and protect me. Amen.

Trust in the LORD with all your heart and do not lean on your own understanding. In all your ways acknowledge Him, and He will make your paths straight.
PROVERBS 3:5–6 NASB

Day 26

WHO AM I?

God, I am trying to figure out who I am and where I fit into this wide world around me. These things I *do* know: Ephesians 1:5 says that You adopted me into Your family—that I belong to You! I am not only Your child (John 1:12), but also Your friend (John 15:15), a new creation (2 Corinthians 5:17), and righteous and holy (Ephesians 4:24). Ephesians 2 describes how my sin kept me separated from You, but through Your Son I am drawn as close to You as possible. Because of Jesus, I am so much more than I could ever dream of being on my own! Help me live with confidence in who I am *in You*. Amen.

But you are the ones chosen by God, chosen for the high calling of priestly work, chosen to be a holy people, God's instruments to do his work and speak out for him, to tell others of the night-and-day difference he made for you— from nothing to something, from rejected to accepted.

1 PETER 2:9 MSG

Day 27
AMAZING LOVE

It's so hard for me to wrap my head around the idea that You, Father—a big God, the Creator of the universe—could love and care for me *even when I mess up!* You breathed life into the land, the seas, and me. Your handiwork is all around, and it's amazing . . .like the first snowfall of the season when I trudge knee-deep through mounds of fluffy stuff or when the flowers and trees bud in the springtime. To think that You—the same God who made all of that—love me is beyond my comprehension. Thank You, Father, for Your constant, unchanging love. Amen

---

When I gaze to the skies and meditate on Your creation—
on the moon, stars, and all You have made, I can't help but
wonder why You care about mortals—sons and daughters
of men specks of dust floating about the cosmos.
PSALM 8:3–4 VOICE

Day 28
COPYCAT

Lord, I look around at school and at the mall, and I see everyone trying to fit in. They copy the styles and actions of the people they think have it all. I get really confused, because I want to fit in too. But I want to please You even more. Give me a strong desire to please You with a full and thankful heart, knowing that Your plan for me is best no matter what all the other people in my life are doing. I want to be transformed by You into a new person—a young woman whose face is radiant and never covered in shame (Psalm 34:5). Amen.

And so, dear brothers and sisters, I plead with you to give your bodies to God because of all he has done for you. Let them be a living and holy sacrifice—the kind he will find acceptable. This is truly the way to worship him. Don't copy the behavior and customs of this world, but let God transform you into a new person by changing the way you think.

Romans 12:1–2 NLT

Day 29
I'M LISTENING TO YOU!

Father, I want the time I spend with You to be moments when I listen to what You have to say, rather than giving You a list of things *I* need and want. I want to be better at listening to You. No, it may not be an audible voice, but You can speak in so many ways. You can point out sins that I've forgotten about. You can bring someone to mind who I need to pray for or even someone who I need to share with who doesn't know You yet. Please help me to be quiet and listen for Your voice. Amen.

If you call out for insight and raise your voice for understanding, if you seek it like silver and search for it as for hidden treasures, then you will understand the fear of the LORD and find the knowledge of God.
PROVERBS 2:3–5 ESV

Day 30
COLLECTING THINGS

Lord, You have told us not to store up treasures on earth but to store up treasures in heaven because the things of earth do not last. But it's so hard to remember that when I see a beautiful pair of earrings or the latest smartphone! Remind me that the things I possess don't have any lasting value and will not bring me closer to You. My purpose in life shouldn't be to collect the biggest and the best things the world has to offer; it should be to glorify You in everything I say and do. Thank You for providing for me emotionally and spiritually as well as physically. Amen.

Then he said to them, "Watch out! Be on your guard against all kinds of greed; life does not consist in an abundance of possessions."
LUKE 12:15 NIV

Day 31
THANKFUL FOR
MY FAMILY

Lord, thank You for parents who love me and guide me and siblings who laugh with me and encourage me. And thank You for grandparents, cousins, aunts, and uncles. You have provided me with such a great support system. I know there are people out there who aren't as blessed in this area as I am. I pray that You would be their family and their support, that they would turn to You and feel You in their lives. Help me to be aware of people like that in my life and to reach out and love them and be their family. Thank You for being my heavenly Father and watching out for me. Amen.

---

*"Respect your father and mother. And love
others as much as you love yourself."*
MATTHEW 19:19 CEV

Day 32
EVEN WHEN. . .

I know I'm supposed to honor my parents, Lord. I know it's the right thing to do. But some days, it's so hard! Even when I don't understand them, I'm supposed to love and obey them. Even when they speak to me in anger, I'm supposed to speak to them with gentleness and deep respect. Even when it seems like they are strangers to me, who don't have a clue about what's going on in my mind and heart. . .even then, I'm supposed to treat them with honor. Help me, Lord, to honor You by honoring my parents, even when it's the last thing I want to do. Help me honor them anyway. Amen.

"Honor your father and mother."
Ephesians 6:2 niv

Day 33
FINDING GOD

Lord, I talk to You all the time, but sometimes I don't know if You're there. But You said You're everywhere. When I hear birds sing, You're there. When a friend shows me kindness, You're there. But You're not just there in the good things. That means when my friends make fun of me and the tears just won't stop, You're there. When someone I love dies. . .You are there. I know You are there, Lord, even though I can't see You. When I look for You, I'll find You because You promised to never leave me. Thank You, Amen.

*"You will seek me and find me when you
seek me with all your heart."*
JEREMIAH 29:13 NIV

Day 34
TO-DOS

Father God, I have read in Your Word that "a good woman is hard to find." Yet that's exactly what I want to become—a good woman. One who does her best with everything she puts her hand to. One who doesn't just play around. One who starts her day with an eager desire to please You—not herself—and ends her day feeling good about everything. Lead my hands to do something more worthwhile, God. Help me make better use of my time. Begin growing me into a woman who pleases *You*—and in the end herself—in every way, every day. Amen.

A good woman is hard to find, and worth
far more than diamonds.
PROVERBS 31:10 MSG

Day 35
GUARDING MY HEART

Help me to remember that it is important to guard my heart, Lord. It seems that so many people and things are tugging at it. When I take a good look, I realize how worldly it all is. I want my heart to be focused on my walk with You first and foremost, above anything else that tries to steal my attention. Teach me to be careful with the word *love*. I use it too freely: "I *love* this dress!" or "I *love* that kind of pizza!" Create in me a desire to place You above all else in my life. You are my God and my Savior. I love You, Lord. Amen.

Above all else, guard your heart,
for everything you do flows from it.
PROVERBS 4:23 NIV

Day 36

DO WHAT'S RIGHT

Lord, help me remember that You honor and reward what is right and that there is punishment for wrongdoing—even if I can't see it. The book of Job says that "the godless seem like a lush plant growing in the sunshine" but "its roots grow down through a pile of stones" and "when it is uprooted, it's as though it never existed" (Job 8:16–18 NLT). I want to please and honor You, God. Help me to not look at others but at You. Help me follow and obey Your Word. Amen.

"But look, God will not reject a person of integrity, nor will he lend a hand to the wicked. He will once again fill your mouth with laughter and your lips with shouts of joy."
JOB 8:20–21 NLT

Day 37
THE ROYAL RULE

When a friend treats me badly, Lord, I often want to get even. I usually talk to another friend about my feelings, but then that turns into a bad-mouthing session, which doesn't end well either. I really want to change how I handle my hurt feelings. Help me to give others grace and to realize that just maybe they've had a bad day and really didn't mean to treat me badly in the first place. Forgive me for jumping to conclusions just because I think someone has rejected or hurt me. Thank You that the Bible gives me clear instructions on what to do when I lose my way—or my tongue! Amen.

Don't bad-mouth each other, friends.
It's God's Word, his Message, his Royal Rule,
that takes a beating in that kind of talk.
JAMES 4:11 MSG

Day 38

WISDOM FROM OUR GENEROUS GOD

Heavenly Father, will You search my heart and show me the things in my life that are getting in the way of my relationship with You? I'm confused about some things, and I'd really like to hear from You about them. Please be generous with me and pour out Your wisdom into my heart. I know I haven't done anything to deserve Your generosity, but I accept that Jesus Christ died for me, and through His power, I am considered a precious daughter of Yours. That is amazing! Thank You, Father! Please show me the way I should go (Psalm 32:8).

If you need wisdom, ask our generous
God, and he will give it to you.

JAMES 1:5 NLT

Day 39
GODLY CHARACTER

Heavenly Father, I do my best to obey You. I know most of the "rules." I shouldn't cheat, I shouldn't lie, I shouldn't misuse Your name, I should honor my parents. . . . I want to be known as a person of character. I want to make the right choices simply because it's the right thing to do, no matter who would see it. . .or if anyone would see it at all. But You see everything, and more than pleasing anyone else, I want to please You the most! Amen.

"The Lord spared me because I did what was right.
Because I have not done evil, he has rewarded me."
2 Samuel 22:21 NCV

Day 40
GO FOR
THE GUSTO

Lord, help me remember that I'm setting an example for others, whether I'm doing the right thing or the wrong thing! Whenever I'm feeling a little lazy—and I know we all do at times—give me the energy to get up and go for the gusto! You're a hard worker, Lord! You created the whole earth in one week's time! You still work hard every single day, taking care of people and making sure we're okay. Show me how to be a hard worker like You, Father, one who never ever gives up, even when the going gets tough! Amen.

Being lazy is no different from being a troublemaker.
PROVERBS 18:9 CEV

Day 41
LOVING MY SIBLINGS

Lord, my siblings are so annoying sometimes! When I'm feeling like this, remind me of why I love them and how they have blessed me. Give me patience with them, and give them patience with me. As we continue life together, I pray that You would bless our relationships with each other and that we would encourage each other to follow You. Not everyone gets a sibling, and even when I'm frustrated with them, I need to be thankful that I've had someone to share my childhood with. Thank You for blessing me with such a great family. Amen.

Respect everyone, and love the family of
believers. Fear God, and respect the king.
1 PETER 2:17 NLT

Day 42

MIRROR, MIRROR ON THE WALL

Lord, sometimes I look at my reflection in the mirror and think I'm pretty. Other times I look away because I feel so ugly. Help me to see that beauty doesn't have anything to do with how I look on the outside. When You look at me, You see one of Your daughters, a lovely princess. And speaking of beauty, Father, would you give me a beautiful heart? Sometimes I let bad attitudes and thoughts mess it up. But I want a beautiful heart so I can shine like a bright light for You. May I always reflect Your beauty, Father! Amen.

Charm can be deceiving, and beauty fades away, but a woman who honors the LORD deserves to be praised.
PROVERBS 31:30 CEV

Day 43
SERVING OTHERS

Father, I remember reading in the Bible about how Jesus healed people when He was on earth. He was kind to everyone; He didn't look down on others because of their challenges. He loved people because they were created in God's image and because they were important despite their problems. God, give me a heart of love for people who live with challenges I can't even begin to understand. Help me discover ways to notice them and make them feel loved. Remind me that my healthy hands and feet and mind are to be used to bless others. Give me a servant's heart. In Jesus' name, amen.

Serve one another humbly in love.
GALATIANS 5:13 NIV

Day 44
GOSSIP

Dear Lord, talking about others is so easy. Sometimes I don't even think about it until after I leave a conversation and consider what I've said. Whenever I'm in a situation where people are gossiping, help me to practice self-control and either keep my mouth closed or come up with something positive to say. I want the words that come out of my mouth to be encouraging and to lift others up, not tear them down and discourage them. I want to be known for speaking kind words and being a trustworthy friend. Help me to love others with the words that come out of my mouth. Amen.

---

*Gossip is no good! It causes hard feelings
and comes between friends.*
PROVERBS 16:28 CEV

Day 45
YOU MADE ME

God, it seems like every time I glance in a mirror I find some-thing I'd like to change about myself. But then I am reminded that You created me. You put me together in my mother's womb. You decided what color my hair and eyes would be. You formed me to be just the size and shape I am, and You blessed me with gifts and abilities that are unique just to me. In a way, I guess I am insulting You when I wish to look a dif-ferent way. You made me just the way You saw fit, God, and You don't make mistakes. So, help me to be the very best me I can be. . .for You!

"Bring to me all the people who are mine, whom I made for my glory, whom I formed and made."
ISAIAH 43:7 NCV

Day 46
THE RIGHT ROAD

I have a guilty conscience, Lord. I was asked a question the other day, and I didn't give a completely honest answer. I know there is no excuse for lying—whether it is to protect a friend or even myself. So right here and now, I am confessing that I did something wrong. And I am asking for Your forgiveness. I know that talking this out with You is only the first step. Now I need to fess up to those I have hurt with my lies. Give me the courage to right whatever I've done wrong. Give me another chance to be faithful to You and Your Word. Amen.

Truth will last forever; lies are soon found out.
PROVERBS 12:19 CEV

Day 47
A BRAND-NEW DAY

Lord, I can't wait to see what wonderful things the day will bring with You by my side! If something bad happens, help me to rejoice in it. I want to praise You *always*—not just when everything goes right, but during difficult times too. Sometimes praising You is a choice I have to make, and not a feeling. Father God, I *choose* to give You the praise You deserve. So today, my prayer is that You will keep my heart fixed on You and my words overflowing with thanksgiving and gratitude for all that You've done and all that You mean to me. Thank You for new beginnings and new opportunities to show my appreciation for all You do. Amen.

This is the day which the LORD hath made;
we will rejoice and be glad in it.
PSALM 118:24 KJV

Day 48
TOO MANY TRIALS

Heavenly Father, the problems I'm going through right now feel like too much for me to handle on my own. Help me to trust in You more and focus on my problems less. Please give me Your peace and strength in the middle of all this stress so that my light will shine for You and my faith will grow. Will You help me understand what it means to have joy during trials? I don't really feel very happy with all that's going on, but I can trust that You are in control of all the things in my life. I trust You. Amen.

Consider it pure joy, my brothers and sisters, whenever you face trials of many kinds, because you know that the testing of your faith produces perseverance.
JAMES 1:2–3 NIV

Day 49
I'M AFRAID

Lord, I feel so much better when I put my trust in You and let You take care of my fears and burdens. Please help me not to fear. Help me trust You more. Forgive me for my lack of faith about certain things. Remind me of the verse "perfect love drives out fear" (1 John 4:18 NIV) when I'm frozen and afraid. And comfort me with Jesus' words to His disciples when faced with a fierce storm on the sea: "Don't be afraid. . . . Take courage. I am here!" (Matthew 14:27 NLT).

So Peter went over the side of the boat and walked on the water toward Jesus. But when he saw the strong wind and the waves, he was terrified and began to sink.
MATTHEW 14:29–30 NLT

Day 50
"FRENEMIES"

Lord, whenever I go through something hard with a friend, please show me how to react in a godly way. It breaks Your heart when we pretend to be friends but then treat each other badly. I know Your Son, Jesus, went through friendship problems too. One of His best friends betrayed Him. That must've really hurt Him! Still, Jesus forgave him. So, help me forgive whenever people go behind my back and do things that bring me pain. I want to learn from Your example, Lord. Help me to be a good friend to others, even when they don't treat me the way I want to be treated. No frenemies here, Lord! Amen.

To speak evil of no one, to avoid quarreling, to be gentle, and to show perfect courtesy toward all people.
TITUS 3:2 ESV

Day 51
BORING?
IGNORING?

Lord, would You please help me not only to listen but to learn from the people You've put in my life? You put them in my life for a reason, and they have so much to teach me! I don't want to be someone who ignores others; I want to be a girl who cares about what people have to say so that people will care about what I have to say! And help me to listen to Your Word too. I need to pay careful attention because You have so much to teach me. Amen.

"Now then, my children, listen to me;
blessed are those who keep my ways.
Listen to my instruction and be wise;
do not disregard it."
PROVERBS 8:32–33 NIV

Day 52
LOVING MYSELF

Lord, I occasionally find it hard to love myself and appreciate all the gifts and talents that You have given me. I tend to focus on the negative, how I wish I were more like some of my friends and siblings, or I focus on all the things I would change about myself if I were given the chance. I need to remember that I am fearfully and wonderfully made by Your hand—there is no one else that You made like me. I trust that You will use me as You see fit in ways that I might never know about. Thank You for creating me just as I am. Amen.

So God created human beings in his image.
In the image of God he created them.
GENESIS 1:27 NCV

Day 53
CONTROLLING MY TEMPER

Sometimes I have trouble controlling my temper, Lord. Things happen that make me angry, and they happen when I least expect it. At times I don't explode right away, but I hold my anger in. Then it builds and builds until I explode—which makes things worse. I need Your help, Lord. I don't always know how to control my negative emotions. Please teach me; show me how to process my emotions in a positive way that won't hurt others. Give me wisdom and understanding. Help me to respond in love, even when I don't feel like it. And help me to forgive others the way You've forgiven me. Amen.

*Human anger does not produce the
righteousness that God desires.*
JAMES 1:20 NIV

Day 54
GOOD THINGS

Heavenly Father, I know there are things about my future I can't control. I just need to trust You. But there are many things I *can* control—at least a little. I know if I study hard and make good grades, I have a better chance of getting a good job. I know if I honor my parents now, it will teach me to honor and respect a boss later. Help me to make smart choices in the things I can manage. As for the things that are beyond my control, I trust You. I know You love me. I know You are compassionate and kind, and You have good things planned for me. I love You, Lord. Amen.

Guide me in your truth, and teach me,
my God, my Savior. I trust you all day long.
PSALM 25:5 NCV

Day 55
YOUR WORD IS LIGHT

I get busy with my friends and activities, Lord, and I don't spend enough time reading my Bible. Please remind me of the importance of setting aside time for that every day. Even when I take time to read just one psalm or a chapter or two from the Gospels, I feel closer to You throughout my day. You have given me a guidebook, but it is up to me to read it. Help me to appreciate Your Word and to seek wisdom from its pages. I love You, Lord, and I want to walk with You all the days of my life. Amen.

Your word is a lamp that gives light wherever I walk.
PSALM 119:105 CEV

Day 56
WHAT DO I DO NOW?

God, help me to recognize Your way for me—to do what will please You, not others. Happiness is temporary. Joy—which comes from You—lasts forever. Help me make wise decisions in my life. Wisdom from Your Word brings success. It will bring more than I can hope for if I follow it instead of choosing my own path. Wisdom is using good judgment. It is more than doing what others around me are doing or telling me I should do. It goes beyond just "following the crowd." Help me to make good decisions, Lord—decisions that will please You. Amen.

Wisdom is far more valuable than rubies.
Nothing you desire can compare with it.
PROVERBS 8:11 NLT

Day 57
ALL I REALLY NEED

Father, please help me to have courage and understand my feelings of low self-esteem aren't based on truth. Help me to see myself through Your loving eyes. Remind me that what others think of me is *not* what defines me. All I really need is Your love and acceptance, and I already have that! When I start feeling bad about myself and the devil bombards me with negative thoughts, please encourage me with a calm, well-balanced mind. Help me to remember that I am of great worth to You, and that's really all that matters. Amen.

God did not give us a spirit of timidity (of cowardice, of craven and cringing and fawning fear), but [He has given us a spirit] of power and of love and of calm and well-balanced mind and discipline and self-control.
2 Timothy 1:7 ampc

Day 58
NEVER EVER,
EVER GIVE UP!

Lord, Your Word encourages me in Isaiah 40:27–31 (NLT):

O Jacob, how can you say the LORD does not see your troubles? O Israel, how can you say God ignores your rights? Have you never heard? Have you never understood? The LORD is the everlasting God, the Creator of all the earth. He never grows weak or weary. No one can measure the depths of his understanding. He gives power to the weak and strength to the powerless. Even youths will become weak and tired, and young men will fall in exhaustion. But those who trust in the LORD will find new strength. They will soar high on wings like eagles. They will run and not grow weary. They will walk and not faint. Amen.

Then Jesus told his disciples. . .they should always pray and not give up.
LUKE 18:1 NIV

Day 59
MAKE ME PURE

God, please help me to be pure. I don't want to do it just to follow a set of rules; I want to do it because You have asked me to. You don't tell us to do things because You don't want us to have fun; You give instruction because that's the only way that will benefit us the most, and that will result in the *best* fun! Thank You, Lord, that even though I may allow impurity into my life at times, I can always tell You I'm sorry. You will forgive me, and You won't hold it against me. I love You, Father. Amen.

How can a young [woman] keep [her] way pure?
By guarding it according to your word.
PSALM 119:9 ESV

Day 60
RESPECTING MY PARENTS

Heavenly Father, it's hard to respect and appreciate my parents sometimes. Even though they have provided for me and love me unconditionally, I still find myself annoyed and wanting to yell at them when I don't get my way or am embarrassed by something they do. Thank You for providing me with such wonderful parents. Help me to come up with ways to show them my respect and appreciation. You are the perfect parent, Lord. Even though my earthly parents aren't perfect, I have You, and I am so thankful for Your presence in my life. Amen.

"Each of you must show great respect for your mother and father, and you must always observe my Sabbath days of rest. I am the LORD your God."
LEVITICUS 19:3 NLT

Day 61
ENCOURAGING OTHERS

Dear Lord, I am not always as encouraging as I should be. I know I can do better. Help me to give generously of my time and talents to those who need them and give me encouragement as well. I know it isn't possible to always have positive things to say, but I believe that You have called me to look at things hopefully and to live a life of joy. So, with that in mind, sustain me when I'm feeling down and show me how to encourage others genuinely, with honesty and with cheerfulness. Amen.

If we can encourage others, we should encourage them. If we can give, we should be generous. If we are leaders, we should do our best. If we are good to others, we should do it cheerfully.
ROMANS 12:8 CEV

Day 62
INNER VS. OUTER BEAUTY

Father, I know that I spend way too much time on how I look. You, on the other hand, focus on inner beauty. Your Word tells me to not be so concerned about the exterior, but to clothe myself with inner beauty. I want to do that, Lord. Remind me to pray more and worry less. Help me to allow You to change the attitudes or thoughts I have that are ugly and displease You. Give me a spiritual makeover! Change me inside. I want Your beauty to shine through me from the inside out because a beautiful spirit radiates even on bad hair days! Amen.

And I want women to be modest in their appearance.
They should wear decent and appropriate clothing and
not draw attention to themselves by the way they fix their
hair or by wearing gold or pearls or expensive clothes.
For women who claim to be devoted to God should make
themselves attractive by the good things they do.
1 TIMOTHY 2:9–10 NLT

Day 63

CARING FOR GOD'S PLANET EARTH

God, thank You for the world You created. I'm glad for grass and trees and flowers and meadows and forests and mountains; I like rivers and lakes and oceans. You made a pretty place for us to live, and I want to say thank You. I want to honor You by being responsible in caring for Your earth, but not worshipping it. Worship belongs to You alone. Help me take care of what You created by doing my part. I love the big world You made, and I know that You will keep it right on going until the time You decide. Thank You that I can trust You. Amen.

The sea is His, for He made it;
and His hands formed the dry land.
PSALM 95:5 NKJV

Day 64
A TIME OF GROWING

Maturing is difficult, God; I'm discovering that. But I'm learning to take my problems to You, and this is a big one for me. What does Your Word say about times like this when it seems life is just crazy, and I don't know when it will get better? Are there answers? I know that people in the Bible were once young like me. Guide me to the places in Your Word that will encourage me and give me hope that this process won't last forever. Help me to believe that You are at work in me. In Christ's name, amen.

He has made everything beautiful in its time.
ECCLESIASTES 3:11 NKJV

Day 65
SHARING MY FAITH

God, Your words are for all believers, not just "advanced" Christians. You have given me the Great Commission. It is Your command that I "make disciples." Show me, Father, what this means for a young person like me. Give me strength to speak about my faith even when it may not be the popular thing to do. I'm afraid I will say it all wrong, but I know the message is a simple one. Please give me the wisdom and the words I need. I cannot witness to others about Christ in my own strength, but I am willing to try if You will help me. Amen.

"Go therefore and make disciples of all nations, baptizing them in the name of the Father and of the Son and of the Holy Spirit, teaching them to observe all that I have commanded you. And behold, I am with you always, to the end of the age."
MATTHEW 28:19–20 ESV

Day 66

A THANKFUL HEART

Lord, I know You tell us to "be thankful in all circumstances" (1 Thessalonians 5:18 NLT), but that is so hard to do when things in my life are not going right. I can't do it on my own! I can be thankful for who You are and for all You have done for me—that I am a part of Your family now and that You care for Your own. I can rejoice in knowing that even when I can't understand my situation, You know all about it. Lord, I am thankful that nothing surprises You and that in every situation You can make good things come from bad circumstances. Amen.

---

*Sing praises to the LORD, you who belong
to him; praise his holy name.*
PSALM 30:4 NCV

Day 67
STINKIN' THINKIN'

Lord, Your scriptures tell me to fill my mind with beauty and truth. You call attention to inner beauty rather than outer beauty. Please help me to turn my negative thinking around. Shift my thought life to everything that is good, honorable, and true to avoid the traps of stinkin' thinkin'! When I think about You and how much You love me, I'm so amazed. Thank You, Father, for loving me so much and thinking only good thoughts about me! Amen.

Finally, brothers and sisters, fill your minds with beauty and truth. Meditate on whatever is honorable, whatever is right, whatever is pure, whatever is lovely, whatever is good, whatever is virtuous and praiseworthy.

PHILIPPIANS 4:8 VOICE

Day 68
ROLE MODEL

I'm not old enough to be considered a role model, am I, Lord? But if I think about it, there are people who could look up to me and want to be like me: younger siblings, kids in the neighborhood, children at church. . .So, I need to consider whether my words and actions are worth imitating. Have I been a good reflection of You? Am I truly someone a younger person should be like? Lord Jesus, please help my words and actions be ones that bring honor to Your name. Please help me to be a good example to those who are younger than I am. Amen.

Let no one despise or think less of you because of your youth, but be an example (pattern) for the believers in speech, in conduct, in love, in faith, and in purity.
1 TIMOTHY 4:12 AMPC

Day 69
PRAYING FOR OTHERS

Thank You, Lord Jesus, for the sacrifice and devotion of people who have positively affected my life. I ask that You bless them for their kindness. Please bring them to my mind so that I can not only be thankful for them, but also ask You to work in their lives. Help me also to love those who have caused me pain and sadness. I don't want to avoid praying for them, Father, because of how they have treated me. I want to talk with You about them because I might be the only one who stops to pray for them today. Thank You for hearing my prayers, Lord. Amen.

I urge you, first of all, to pray for all people. Ask God to help them; intercede on their behalf, and give thanks for them.
1 TIMOTHY 2:1 NLT

Day 70
ME? JEALOUS?

Lord, sometimes I'm jealous of other people. I'm not just jealous of the things they have, I'm also jealous of the way they look or the kind of house they live in. I'm even jealous of their friendships. I don't want to be like this. Jealousy is a sin. I know that, and I'm working on it! Please help me get rid of it. I don't want to be selfish. And I don't want to compare myself with others. I know you can change my heart and get rid of these feelings I have. I choose to lay down my "I want what she has" attitude today, Lord. Take my heart and make it clean in Your sight. Amen.

But if you are bitterly jealous and there is selfish ambition in your heart, don't cover up the truth with boasting and lying.
JAMES 3:14 NLT

Day 71
STRONG AND COURAGEOUS

Can You make me strong, Lord? I know the Bible says You can! You say that I can be strong and courageous, like David facing the giant Goliath! But even David didn't have the courage to slay Goliath on his own. He needed Your strength, Father. That's what I'm asking for today—Your strength. I put on Your armor and take up my sword and shield (my Bible) and march forward like a brave warrior, headed into the enemy's camp. I know You will go before me, and that gives me all the courage I need. With Your help, I will be victorious! Amen.

"Be strong and very courageous. Be careful to obey all the law my servant Moses gave you; do not turn from it to the right or to the left, that you may be successful wherever you go."
JOSHUA 1:7 NIV

Day 72
SEEK PEACE

Girls can be mean, Lord. We're supposed to be all pink and fluffy and sweet, but we have a vicious side too. I'd like to say I'm innocent of this behavior, but I'm not, Lord. I'm not proud of it, and I don't want to be that way. I want to be a peacemaker. I want to help everyone get along, not contribute to the fighting. But I don't always know what to do or how to act or what to say to make things better. I need Your help, Lord. Give me Your wisdom today and every day, to know how to bring peace to difficult situations. Amen.

Seek peace and pursue it.
PSALM 34:14 NIV

Day 73
THOUGHTS ABOUT ROMANCE

Father, I've been thinking about romance; it will be cool to fall in love with a great guy. I want to have my own romance someday. In the fairy tales, the princesses are loved by strong, handsome princes. I want to fall in love with a wonderful man and have a beautiful wedding day and live happily ever after. I ask You to help me know the man that You want me to marry; help me guard my heart and not just give it away to anyone. And thank You that even if I never marry, I can be loved by You, and that love will last forever. Amen.

"Yes, I have loved you with an everlasting love."
JEREMIAH 31:3 NKJV

Day 74
HEALING POWER

I want to offer a prayer today, Jesus, for sick friends and family members. I know that You healed so many people when You were here. So I ask You now, Lord, to apply that same healing power to the ones I love. I trust in You and surrender my worries. I am putting their lives into Your big, strong, mighty hands. Increase the faith of my loved ones who are hurting. And if they don't know You, I pray that their eyes would be opened. That they would see You for who You truly are—a great and loving God. Thank You, Lord. Amen.

He heals the brokenhearted and bandages their wounds.
PSALM 147:3 NLT

Day 75
GOD'S LOVE

God, thank You for assuring me through Your Word that nothing about You ever changes. No matter where I go, You are there. No matter what changes take place in my life, one thing will remain steadfast, and that is the deep love You have for me. When I am afraid, remind me of Your love. Comfort me and teach me to run to You when my heart is troubled or when I feel like life is spinning out of control. Thank You, Lord, for loving me with a love that will truly never let me go. Amen.

I am sure that nothing can separate us from God's love—not life or death, not angels or spirits, not the present or the future, and not powers above or powers below. Nothing in all creation can separate us from God's love for us in Christ Jesus our Lord!
ROMANS 8:38–39 CEV

Day 76
GOD WILL NEVER LEAVE ME

People fail me, Father. My friends don't always understand me; my family can't be there for me every single moment; and teachers and other adults may not follow through on their promises. No one is perfect except You, God. You will always be there for me. On days when I feel forgotten or overlooked, remind me that I can count on You, Lord. You won't leave me. You won't abandon me. Help me to know I am not alone. I can always reach out to You in prayer. Thank You for being the one I can turn to, for being there for me even when others are not available. Amen.

God has said, "I will never leave you; I will never abandon you."
HEBREWS 13:5 NCV

Day 77
GUIDE ME, LORD

I'm so confused, Lord. My thoughts run this way and that, and I don't know what to think sometimes. There are days when I need some solid advice and guidance. Okay, I admit I need guidance *most* of the time! Thank You that Your direction is perfect and Your judgments are wise. I praise You for the guidance You give me daily as I seek You in prayer. It amazes me that You often give me wisdom beyond my years! Lord, I want to follow You and continue to seek Your will and ways throughout my lifetime. Please guide me on the pathway You've set just for me. Amen.

The LORD says, "I will guide you along the best pathway for your life. I will advise you and watch over you."
PSALM 32:8 NLT

Day 78
GOD HEARS ME

Hello, God? Can You really hear me? Sometimes I feel like my prayers are not making their way to You. I want to have a deep relationship with You, knowing that You are a constant presence in my life. Speak to me through Your Word. It amazes me that when I read and memorize Your Word, You bring it to my mind later at just the right time when I need to hear from You. This helps me trust that You really do hear me and care about all the little and big things in my life. Thank You for hearing me, Father. Amen.

Out of my distress I called on the LORD;
the LORD answered me and set me free.
PSALM 118:5 ESV

Day 79
CHANGING MY WORLD

Father, I want to do great things for You! There are so many people with big needs all around me. Some are in desperate need of financial help. Others could really use my help in doing physical work that they are unable to do themselves. Some would benefit from me volunteering my time in service. And others just need a friend who can sit and listen to them. Help me to be aware of people in my world who I could assist. And then give me the strength to help them out—not to receive recognition but rather to be a light for You. Amen.

Do not neglect to do good and to share what you have, for such sacrifices are pleasing to God.

HEBREWS 13:16 ESV

Day 80
WONDERFULLY MADE

Father, I need to stop and think about the things I'm putting in my body. And sometimes I don't really feel like exercising or taking care of myself. I'm too tired or too busy. But You made me, Lord, and I know You want me to take care of myself. The Bible says that I'm "fearfully and wonderfully" made, which means I'm important to You. I guess that also means that I should take care of my body so that it will stay healthy and strong. I want to live a long life and be healthy and strong, so help me to be mindful of what I eat and to exercise so that I can achieve those goals! Amen.

---

*I praise you because I am fearfully and wonderfully
made; your works are wonderful, I know that full well.*
PSALM 139:14 NIV

Day 81
BIG AND LITTLE STRESSES

God, I stress out about so many things. It's easy to come to You with the big stuff because You are a big God and I know that You care. But it's hard for me to bring the little things, because those seem so small in comparison. But I know there is not one problem or complaint I have that is too small for You, because You care about everything in my life. You care for the birds of the air *and* the beasts of the field. Because You take such care with those small creatures, it gives me confidence in Your care of me. Thank You for those examples of Your love and care. Amen.

God, examine me and know my heart;
test me and know my anxious thoughts.
PSALM 139:23 NCV

Day 82
WHEN I'M AFRAID

Sometimes I feel afraid, Lord. But You said if I trust in You, I don't have to be afraid of anything. You'll be with me in everything I do, and You'll help me and protect me. I know I still must make wise choices. I can't do foolish things and expect You to protect me. But I also know that if I'm following Your lead, You'll never leave me. And even when harm comes my way, You'll help me through it. I don't have to fear as long as I'm trusting You and holding on to Your promises. Lord, please replace my fear with a calm assurance that You have everything under control. Amen.

When I am afraid, I put my trust in you.
PSALM 56:3 NIV

Day 83
KEEPING THINGS ORDERLY

Chores, God? I don't like them—making my bed, loading the dishwasher, running the vacuum, doing the laundry. I confess I don't always have a good attitude when my mom asks me to help her, and I'm sorry about that. I really need Your help not to be grumpy about my chores. When my mom needs me to help her, I want to be cheerful and not complain. Remind me that I am pleasing You when I obey and when I keep things in their place. And I'm sure glad I can trust You to keep all the big stuff running correctly! Amen.

He existed before anything else,
and he holds all creation together.
COLOSSIANS 1:17 NLT

Day 84
A UNIQUE PURPOSE

Lord, You have created me for a unique purpose. You have set me here at this exact time, space, and place for a reason. And, although I am not sure yet what that is, I know that one day You will show me exactly what You've had in mind for me all along. Help me not to worry about the future too much but to continue to explore this world and my role in it. Help me not to obsess over which road to take because You know exactly where I'm heading and will give me signs along the way—in Your own good time. Meanwhile, I will do my part to be patient, trusting, and watchful. Amen.

"For I know the plans I have for you," declares the LORD, "plans to prosper you and not to harm you, plans to give you hope and a future."
JEREMIAH 29:11 NIV

Day 85
FAMILY

God, You gave me the family I have. And no family is perfect. Help me to appreciate the good things and to change the things I can about myself to help make my family better. The things I can't change are the things I have to trust to You, Father. Right or wrong, there is so much beyond my control. I can only make decisions for myself, not for anyone else. When I become discontent with who I am and where I came from, I want to look for the positive areas of my life. Help me recognize the people You have placed around me to love me and help me. Amen.

Exploit or abuse your family, and end up with a fistful of air; common sense tells you it's a stupid way to live.
Proverbs 11:29 msg

LOOKING GOOD

I care about what others think of me, God, but maybe I should care more about what *You* think of me. Isn't the inside more important than the outside? How I dress matters to me, but what I haven't thought about until recently, God, is that it matters to others and can impact their lives too. I want to look cool, but I understand that modesty is important too. Luke 12:27 tells us that You "clothed" the lilies in the field, and they are beautiful! Maybe what I am wearing matters most of all to You, God. Help me find clothes that I like but that are also pleasing to You. Amen.

"Don't fuss about what's on the table at mealtimes or if the clothes in your closet are in fashion. There is far more to your inner life than the food you put in your stomach, more to your outer appearance than the clothes you hang on your body."
LUKE 12:22–24 MSG

Day 87
GOD GIVES
ME STRENGTH

What does it mean to be strong, Father? I cry when someone hurts my feelings or when things go wrong in my life. I don't mean to pout or act like a baby, but sometimes I let my emotions get the best of me. Only You can give me the strength to stand fearless in uncomfortable situations. Help me to grow stronger each day—physically, spiritually, and emotionally—so that I can be the person You created me to be. Give me victory over life's fears and frustrations. To know that I can walk in Your strength is a comfort to me. You've put a song in my heart and victory in my steps. Amen.

The LORD is my strength and my song; he has given me victory.
PSALM 118:14 NLT

Day 88

BEAUTIFUL INSIDE
AND OUT

There are so many people I would consider beautiful, Lord; but in all honesty, there are days when I don't feel like anyone could use the word *beautiful* to describe me. Forgive me, Father, for judging my worth by what my hair or face looks like, how much I weigh, or the kind of clothes I wear. You are the master artist and have designed me just the way I am. Please don't let me get so caught up in the world's standard of beauty. Help me to focus on being what I need to be in Your eyes, not to the eyes of those around me. Amen.

---

*"Looks aren't everything. . . . GOD judges persons
differently than humans do. Men and women
look at the face; GOD looks into the heart."*
1 SAMUEL 16:7 MSG

Day 89
I LOVE YOU, LORD!

Father, it's so easy to say I love something or someone. But God, I *really* do love You. You have made me unique, and You have promised to meet my needs. I can trust You with my deepest secrets and know that You not only hear me, but care about me too. You only want what's best for me. Thank You for loving me first, and for loving me so much that You sent Your Son to die for me. I'm sorry for the times I don't show my love and seem to take our relationship for granted. My heart is full of love for You, and I want to grow in my love for You more every day. Amen.

"Love the Lord your God with all your heart and with all your soul and with all your mind and with all your strength."
MARK 12:30 NIV

Day 90
CARING FOR
THOSE IN NEED

Lord, give me eyes to see the needs of people all around me—the elderly neighbor who needs a friend. The little boy with cancer. The lady across the street who has no time to spend with her kids because she's always working. How can You use me to help out? Can I offer to clean? To fix a meal? To start a fundraiser? Whatever You ask me to do, Father, I will do! I want to reach out to those in need as You've told me in Your Word to do. Amen.

Suppose a brother or a sister is without clothes and daily food. If one of you says to them, "Go in peace; keep warm and well fed," but does nothing about their physical needs, what good is it? In the same way, faith by itself, if it is not accompanied by action, is dead.

JAMES 2:15–17 NIV

Day 91
STRESS EXPRESS

Between all the schoolwork, sports, fun with friends, stuff with family, and other activities, Lord, I feel super stressed out. Please show me how to prioritize my activities, beginning with what's most important spending time with You. When I feel frazzled and depleted of energy, lead me to Your side. I know You have a place where I can be at rest, where all is still. In Your presence, I can get things straight in my head. I find new direction and strength. I am refueled. Here, I am at peace. Here I am—with You. Amen.

He makes me lie down in [fresh, tender] green pastures;
He leads me beside the still and restful waters.
He refreshes and restores my life (my self).
PSALM 23:2–3 AMPC

Day 92
NOT FUNNY

I don't think it's funny to insult people, Lord. It's hurtful to the person being insulted. Even if they laugh on the outside, I know they're hurting inside. I know because it's happened to me. Help me not to fall into the trap of saying mean things just to get a laugh, Lord. I don't want to cause others to hurt the way I've been hurt. I want to be a person people feel safe with, a person people know will be kind no matter what. Teach me to be an encourager. I want to build people up and make them feel good about themselves. Amen.

Therefore encourage one another and build one another up, just as you are doing.
1 Thessalonians 5:11 esv

Day 93
I HATE DIVORCE

God, I know that divorce happens and that it's not the kids' fault. But it is terrible to have a family that is all broken up and must try to be nice to each other in public. I know You made families to stay together, but Satan doesn't want it that way. He is happy when families split up. I'm so glad that You can be there to help hurting families. Thank You for being there to hear prayers and bring comfort. Be with everyone who is hurt today because of divorce. Let Your love be felt. I ask this in Jesus' name, amen.

He heals the brokenhearted and bandages their wounds.
PSALM 147:3 NLT

Day 94
IT'S NOT FAIR!

God, I know Jesus' arms are open wide to everyone. He loves even the unlovable and died for *every* person—even those who hate Him. What's fair about that? God, You are holy. We are not. It is only by Your Son's sacrifice that we can know You. By Your standards we deserve to be separated from You. Yet, because of Your great love for us through Jesus, there is a way we can be with You forever even though we don't deserve it! What's "fair" about that? Lord, thank You that life is not fair—but You are! Thank You for making a way for me to know You through Your Son. Amen.

" 'Still, you keep on saying, "The Master's way
isn't fair." We'll see, Israel. I'll decide on each of
you exactly according to how you live.' "
EZEKIEL 33:20 MSG

Day 95
POPULARITY

I want to be popular, God. I want to be one of the girls everyone admires. I know it may not be the right way to feel, but it's the truth. I long to be part of the "in" crowd, and some days I would do almost anything just to make sure I'm noticed. Clean up this way of thinking in me, God. Show me the right kind of friends—those who love You. And then, if others do notice me, help me point them to You. Help me to not be so worried about being popular. Amen.

The righteous choose their friends carefully,
but the way of the wicked leads them astray.
PROVERBS 12:26 NIV

Day 96
DOING MY BEST

Doing ordinary things well doesn't seem like it amounts to much, Lord, but in Matthew 25 You promise that those who are faithful in the small things will be rewarded. I want to succeed—I want to *be* the best at something. But what if my best isn't good enough—or if I'm not really good at anything? Philippians 4:13 (NKJV) says, "I can do all things through Christ," so then I guess it's not about what I can do, but what You can do through me. So help me do my best for You, Lord—not for others or even myself. Help me to see that the small things are important simply because You say they are. Amen.

---

*Observe people who are good at their work—
skilled workers are always in demand and admired;
they don't take a backseat to anyone.*
PROVERBS 22:29 MSG

Day 97
TRUE SUCCESS

I want to know You more, Father God. I want to be successful not only in my physical life, but in my spiritual life as well. I want You first in my life because that's true success. You said to seek the kingdom of God and Your righteousness, and everything else will fall into place! Please nudge me to read the Bible and spend time with You every day, Lord, before I do anything else. So many things draw me away from quiet time with You. I desire to seek You with all of my heart. And I know that if I do, You will take care of all the other needs in my life. Amen.

"But seek ye first the kingdom of God, and his righteousness; and all these things shall be added unto you."
MATTHEW 6:33 KJV

Day 98
FROM SORROW TO JOY

I'm really sad, Father. Please open Your Word to me. Lead me to a new hope. Give me the courage to keep going. Lift the weight of sorrow from my heart. Help me to take things one moment, one hour, one day at a time, knowing that You are holding my hand through it all. Show me how to praise You, for I know that when I do, I will suddenly feel better. Thank You for what You are going to do in my life and for the joy that will someday be after this sorrow. Amen.

I would have lost heart, unless I had believed that I would see the goodness of the LORD in the land of the living.
PSALM 27:13 NKJV

Day 99
NEVER GIVE UP!

Thank You, heavenly Father, for giving me the strength I need at times when I'm weak. I know what waits for me at the "finish line," but the work getting there wears me out. If I try it on my own, the results aren't usually what I was hoping for. But You have promised to carry me through when it's tough, so I ask for Your help in reaching my goals. I don't want to give up, Lord. Help me keep my eyes on You and on the benefit I will receive from finishing well. In Jesus' name, amen.

Do not let yourselves get tired of doing good. If we do not give up, we will get what is coming to us at the right time.

GALATIANS 6:9 NLV

Day 100
LEAVING A LEGACY

Wow, God! It's so awesome to think that You knew me even before I was born, just like You knew my parents and grandparents before they were born. I guess that must mean You know more about me than anyone, even my own family. That also means I can trust You because You're the one who designed me in the first place. Thank You for taking the time to create me, Lord. I want to leave a legacy, to be remembered as part of something bigger than myself. Help me to do that by the way I live and the way I worship. Amen.

The word of the LORD came to me, saying, "Before I formed you in the womb I knew you, before you were born I set you apart; I appointed you as a prophet to the nations."
JEREMIAH 1:4–9 NIV

Day 101
VOICES

God, sometimes I need time alone, apart from all the voices and chaos of the world. I enjoy spending time by myself in my room where I can focus on my own thoughts. I think about things in my life, and I think about You, Father. When I'm alone is when I hear You the most. It's then that I can open my heart and tell You how I feel. Yours is the only voice I never tire of. It is gentle, soothing, and refreshing to me. I want to hear Your voice more. Lord, as I pray, please help me to listen. When I read the Bible, show me the words I need for my life. Amen.

Be still, and know that I am God.
PSALM 46:10 NKJV

Day 102
A NEW SONG

Some days I find myself complaining about everything, Lord. I don't mean to, but sometimes everything just seems to get on my nerves. Whatever the reason, those days just aren't any fun. But I don't have to complain, do I? I can choose to look for the positive in any situation. You said You'd put a song in my heart if I look to You. That's what I want, Lord. I want to be so content, so filled with Your love that I'm always singing, even if it's just inside my head. Next time I feel like complaining, help me to sing a song of praise instead. Amen.

He put a new song in my mouth,
a hymn of praise to our God.
PSALM 40:3 NIV

Day 103
HONOR YOUR FATHER AND MOTHER

Heavenly Father, *honor* means respect, and *respect* means "paying attention to" or having "a high or special regard for." When I listen and acknowledge what my parents say, I have respect for them. I can honor their position as my parents, and I know I must obey them. Even when my opinion is different from theirs, I need to speak politely and not be angry. That's hard sometimes, Lord. Help me understand what it is to honor and obey my parents without losing my ability to think for myself and to always be respectful. Amen.

Children, do what your parents tell you. This is only right. "Honor your father and mother" is the first commandment that has a promise attached to it, namely, "so you will live well and have a long life."
Ephesians 6:1–3 msg

Day 104
RIGHT HERE, RIGHT NOW

Here I am, Lord, right here, right now. At this moment, I am imagining You sitting right next to me. Forgive me for being so caught up in the world. Give me the peace, strength, direction, and hope I need to live the life You have planned out for me. Help me to be more loving to myself, my family, and my friends. In this moment. . .

I give You my heart—to have and to hold. Cleanse it of worry.

I give You my mind. Fill it with good thoughts.

I give You my life. Lead me where You would have me go.

I give You my all as I rest in Your presence. Speak to me. I'm listening. Amen.

"See! I stand at the door and knock. If anyone hears My voice and opens the door, I will come in to him and we will eat together."
REVELATION 3:20 NLV

Day 105
A MASTERPIECE

I sure don't feel like a masterpiece, God. Sometimes I feel more like a mess! But You gaze at me and smile. I am Your daughter, Your precious child, Your masterpiece. Give me the ability to do the good works that You have created me to do. Show me Your will and Your way for my life and give me courage to follow You even when I'm not sure where You are taking me. I am Yours, God. And wow, it feels amazing to be valued by the God of the universe! Thank You for making me, for loving me, and for stamping me with Your approval—just because I'm me, just because I belong to You. Amen.

For we are God's masterpiece. He has created us anew in Christ Jesus, so we can do the good things he planned for us long ago.
EPHESIANS 2:10 NLT

Day 106
DON'T JUDGE ME

I hate it when people decide things about me that aren't true. They make a "judgment" about my clothes, where I live, the color of my hair or skin, the way I talk or look. They make assumptions about me based on their own false ideas. But if I'm honest, Lord, I might do the same thing. If I'm not careful, I can make judgments about others based on my own biases. I really don't want to do that! Help me to see people for who they really are—not what they look like or even what they do. God, help me to treat others as I want to be treated. Amen.

"Don't judge others, and you will not be judged.
Don't accuse others of being guilty, and you will not be
accused of being guilty. Forgive, and you will be forgiven."
LUKE 6:37 NCV

Day 107
THE TRUTH!

Lord, Your Word tells me that the devil is the father of all lies. But I belong to You. You are my heavenly Father, and I am Your child because Your Spirit lives inside me. Please help me when I'm tempted to lie—no matter how hard it might be to tell the truth. Even in those moments when I'm afraid of the consequences, remind me to do what's right. I ask that my words reflect You, Father. Give me uplifting, honest, caring words as I speak the truth. I surrender my will to You. I surrender my thoughts and words to You too! Amen.

So put away your lies and speak the truth to one another because we are all part of one another.
EPHESIANS 4:25 VOICE

Day 108
A WALK DOWN
THE RUNWAY

I'll admit it, Lord. . .I pay a little too much attention to what people are wearing sometimes. I don't want to get too carried away with it, though. Fashion can be a fun distraction, but it doesn't need to be my main focus. I ask You to remind me daily that it's not what I wear on the outside that matters, but the condition of my heart. Remind me too of all the girls around the globe who don't have money to buy new clothes or shoes. To You, they are just as beautiful, even if they don't have fancy things to wear. Amen.

For women who claim to be devoted to God should make themselves attractive by the good things they do.
1 TIMOTHY 2:10 NLT

Day 109
MY LIFE IS YOURS

Dear Father, I admit that when I hear the word *surrender*, I think of someone who loses because they gave up. It doesn't sound like something a person who is strong and in control would do. I'm sorry for the times I have tried to take things into my own hands and do things without Your help. That never seems to work out for the best. I know the safest place for me to be is in Your care because You see the "big picture" of my life and know what's best for me. I want to surrender my whole life to You. I want You to have complete control. In Your name, amen.

Therefore, I urge you, brothers and sisters, in view of God's mercy, to offer your bodies as a living sacrifice, holy and pleasing to God—this is your true and proper worship.

ROMANS 12:1 NIV

ME AND
MY BIG MOUTH!

Oh, my big mouth! Lord, sometimes it gets me in trouble. I don't mean to spout off, but sometimes I get upset, and things escape my lips before I can even think them through. Forgive me for this, Lord. Help me change. Make my words gentle. May I follow Your example of loving others, showing courtesy to all the people I know. I know that You want me to guard my tongue, Father. I need to know how to react when I'm faced with a situation that's tough. I don't want to spout off. I want to react calmly. And when I do speak, I want my words to be kind and loving, not angry and mean. Amen.

To speak evil of no one, to avoid quarreling, to be gentle, and to show perfect courtesy toward all people.

TITUS 3:2 ESV

Day 111
MY SELFISHNESS

Dear Lord, I can be so very selfish in every area of my life. I am selfish with my time, my possessions, my friends, and a lot of other things. I don't want to constantly think only of myself; I want to be unselfish and serve those around me in any way that I can. You have said that the greatest commandments are to love You and to love my neighbor as myself; help me to do both of those things in my daily life. Thank You for never being selfish and being the perfect example of serving others. Amen.

Do nothing out of selfish ambition or vain conceit. Rather, in humility value others above yourselves, not looking to your own interests but each of you to the interests of the others.
PHILIPPIANS 2:3–4 NIV

Day 112
DELIGHT IN HIM

There are so many things I want, Lord. New clothes, new electronics, new stuff for my room. . .and whenever I get something I want, there's always another item to take its place on my wish list. But You said I'm supposed to want You more than I want anything else. I'm supposed to delight in You. I guess that means You're supposed to be the one who makes me happier than any of my stuff, happier than any of my goals. Help me, today and every day, to delight in You. I know being close to You is the best thing I could ever wish for. Amen.

Take delight in the LORD, and he will give
you the desires of your heart.
PSALM 37:4 NIV

Day 113

GRANDPARENTS
ARE GREAT

God, I wonder if Jesus knew His grandparents. I know it was different for Him because He was really Your Son, but maybe He had a special relationship with His earthly grandparents too. It's really cool that You understand the things about my life that way. So, I'm saying a prayer of thanks for my grandparents and also praying for them. Please take care of them and keep them healthy and let me have them in my life for a long time. Help me to be a good granddaughter. I ask this in Jesus' name, amen.

Grandchildren are the crowning glory of the aged.
<small>Proverbs 17:6 NLT</small>

Day 114

LOVE GOD AND LOVE OTHERS

God, You've made Your purpose for me pretty simple, and I'm so thankful for that! Love You and love others. Help me to focus on that each and every day and not get caught up on rules and laws. I trust that if I'm growing in my love for You and for the people in my life, You will teach me all that I need to know through Your Word and through the people around me that love You too. Thank You, Jesus. I love You. I'll do my best to love others too—with Your help! Amen.

If anyone boasts, "I love God," and goes right on hating his brother or sister, thinking nothing of it, he is a liar. If he won't love the person he can see, how can he love the God he can't see? The command we have from Christ is blunt: Loving God includes loving people. You've got to love both.
1 JOHN 4:20–21 MSG

Day 115

GOD WILL TAKE
CARE OF ME

Lord, the future frightens me. The what-ifs are overwhelming. I try to turn off my brain and not get anxious, but I am really scared at times. How silly of me to think like that! You are the powerful God of the universe, and You have promised to take care of me! You keep the earth spinning on its axis. You clothe the fields with grass, and You even feed the birds. How much more You value me as Your child, created in Your Image! I know that You will be there every step of the way and that if I look to You, You will provide all that I need. Thank You, Lord! Amen.

"Look at the birds. They don't plant or harvest or store
food in barns, for your heavenly Father feeds them.
And aren't you far more valuable to him than they are?"
MATTHEW 6:26 NLT

Day 116
I AM WONDERFUL!

You made me wonderful, Father! Thank You that I can say that, not in an arrogant way—but in a way that gives me confidence to live out a life that pleases You! I don't need to worry about what other people think about me because I know what You think about me, Father God! Everyone else seems to look at outside appearances only, but I feel blessed and deeply loved that You look at the inside of my heart and call me Your daughter. Thanks for making me beautiful in Your eyes—and help me to smile like I believe it! Amen.

"Bring the ones who are called by My name; the ones I made, shaped, and created for My profound glory."
ISAIAH 43:7 VOICE

Day 117
THE "IN" CROWD

Lord, I admit that sometimes I go along with the crowd just so I will be liked and accepted. I want to fit in; and instead of standing up for what's right, I remain silent. That's something You never did, Lord. Help me to seek out other people who have a strong Christian faith. Bring friends into my life who can help strengthen my spiritual growth and not diminish it. Most of all, when I'm around people who don't know You, help me to love them and pray for them. Help me to be a good influence in their lives so they can see how You've made a difference in mine. Amen.

Do not be deceived: "Evil company corrupts good habits."
1 CORINTHIANS 15:33 NKJV

Day 118
EVEN SO,
I PRAISE YOU!

Father God, the Bible tells me I can know one thing for sure about Your will for my life: namely, that I should give thanks in *every* circumstance. Not a particularly easy thing to do because not everything I go through is an awesome experience. In fact, some things in life are just plain awful. Yet You made it clear that I am to show my appreciation to You—no matter what I'm going through—to praise You *in* my circumstance, not *for* it. I know You don't invite bad things into my life, Father; but I can thank You despite them. Today I praise and thank You, no matter what my day brings. Amen.

Give thanks in all circumstances; for this is
the will of God in Christ Jesus for you.
1 THESSALONIANS 5:18 ESV

Day 119
STUDY HELP

Father, I know You want me to do my best in everything I do, which includes my schoolwork. Help me to have a better attitude about it and want to do a good job. The time I put into my schoolwork will determine my grades, so I know that for now I need to work hard to get through my classes. Help me, please, to study what I need to and for the length of time that I should. Please teach me how to avoid distractions so that I can reach my goals and finish well. . .so I can even have some fun time when the work is done. Amen.

Do your best to present yourself to God as one approved, a worker who has no need to be ashamed, rightly handling the word of truth.
2 TIMOTHY 2:15 ESV

Day 120
TOUGH STUFF!

Life is so hard sometimes, Lord! I don't think I have enough energy to get everything done. Schoolwork. After-school activities. Family events. Church obligations. I feel like I'm in over my head. How can I possibly get everything done and still get a good night's sleep? Show me what's important to do, Father. I don't want to do stuff just to stay busy. I want the "stuff" I do to be important to You. So, if there's anything in my life I'm not supposed to be doing, show me. Help me to create a schedule that works for me and my family, one that leaves me plenty of time left over to pray and read Your Word. Amen.

From the ends of the earth, I cry to you for help when my heart is overwhelmed. Lead me to the towering rock of safety.
PSALM 61:2 NLT

Day 121
PRIDE

Dear Lord, help me to be humble. When I take pride in my grades or my success in sports or my appearance, I need to remember that You are the one who has given me these abilities and that I should be humble and thankful for what You have given. I know there is nothing wrong with being confident in the gifts that You have given me, but I don't want to brag and base my self-worth on things that I do. I want to be humble and serve others and glorify You. Amen.

Too much pride can put you to shame. It's wiser to be humble.
PROVERBS 11:2 CEV

Day 122
NOT ALONE

You made me, Lord. You know my thoughts, and You understand things about me that I don't even understand about myself. And since You promised You'd never leave me, that You'll always be with me, I know I don't have to feel alone. I'm always in the company of the one who knows me better than anyone and who loves me just the same. I know Your eyes are always on me, and You always hear me when I talk to You. Walk with me as I go through my day. Whisper Your words into my mind. Remind me of Your presence so I won't have to feel alone. Amen.

The eyes of the LORD are on the righteous,
and his ears are attentive to their cry.
PSALM 34:15 NIV

Day 123
NO MORE DEATH

God, I know that death is the result of sin coming into our world long ago when the first couple, Adam and Eve, disobeyed You. I know You didn't mean for us to die. I wish there weren't funeral homes and caskets and cemeteries. But there are, and I need You to help me deal with it. Thank You for the hope of heaven for those who believe in You. Thank You for sending Your Son to pay for my sins so that I can live forever with You. Give me hope and remind me to trust You. And someday take me to live with You forever. In Jesus' name, amen.

"And God will wipe away every tear from their eyes;
there shall be no more death, nor sorrow, nor crying."
REVELATION 21:4 NKJV

Day 124
PEACE AND HARMONY

I come to You today, Lord, with a troubled heart. How am I to handle bullies? What's a girl to do? Put Your wall of protection around me. Shield me from the hurtful words of others. Give me Your eyes so that I can see the good in all people. And fill me with the strength to lend a helping hand and to lift up those who are weak. I pray for peace—at home, at school, and in our neighborhood. Show us all how to live together in harmony. Amen.

There are six things the LORD hates, seven that are detestable to him: haughty eyes, a lying tongue, hands that shed innocent blood, a heart that devises wicked schemes, feet that are quick to rush into evil, a false witness who pours out lies and a person who stirs up conflict in the community.
PROVERBS 6:16–19 NIV

Day 125
"I'M SORRY"

Lord, there are times when I lose my temper and end up saying things I don't really mean. Then there are other times when I mock someone just to make my friends laugh. What I'm trying to say is that there are situations when I say or do the wrong thing, and an apology on my part is needed. For all these mistakes I've made, please give me the courage to say from my heart, "I'm sorry." Once I have done my part to heal a rift, then, and only then, will I feel ready, willing, and able to come and worship You with a clean heart and a clear conscience. Amen.

"If you enter your place of worship and, about to make an offering, you suddenly remember a grudge a friend has against you, abandon your offering, leave immediately, go to this friend and make things right. Then and only then, come back and work things out with God."
MATTHEW 5:23–24 MSG

Day 126

THAT MAKES
ME SO MAD!

Proverbs 18:21 (MSG) says, "Words kill, words give life; they're either poison or fruit—you choose." I do choose, Lord—even when my emotions can seem out of control, I still have a choice what comes out of my mouth. Help me to say what I want to say without destroying others in the process. I know I hate harsh words when they are directed at me, so help me to speak kindly even when there are difficult things to express. Thank You that I can come to You with what I am feeling, God. I know You understand and can help me handle my anger. Amen.

A gentle answer deflects anger,
but harsh words make tempers flare.

PROVERBS 15:1 NLT

Day 127
ROLE MODELS

Lord, Your servant Paul told the early Christians to follow his example as he followed the example of Christ. I know I should choose Christian role models who live their lives for You. Even though the world bombards me with temptations and influences of the rich and famous, I ask that You change my heart to desire only Your ways and Your will. Surround my life with more of You, Jesus. I want to follow You; I want to be like You. Forgive me for often allowing the world's influences to speak to my heart. Give me godly role models and help me become a good role model too. Amen.

Follow my example, as I follow the example of Christ.
1 CORINTHIANS 11:1 NIV

Day 128
NO MORE COMPARING

Lord, I believe that when You look at me You see something beautiful that You created. You smile at me and are pleased by my appearance. Would You please help me to see myself the way You see me? When I compare myself with my friends, I get very insecure. Please forgive me for that and set my heart and mind back on You. You look into my eyes and call me beautiful. You know the number of hairs on my head (Luke 12:7), and You even count my tears (Psalm 56:8). Thanks, God. My heart belongs to You alone. Amen.

But when they measure themselves by one another and compare themselves with one another, they are without understanding.
2 CORINTHIANS 10:12 ESV

Day 129
DISCIPLINE

It's just not fair, Lord! I shouldn't be grounded! I didn't do anything wrong! But even though I think it's unfair, I need You to help me be respectful—not to try to get an easier punishment, but because You want me to honor those in authority over me. You've put them in that position, so I need to respect that. . . and even be thankful for it. Thank You for giving me people who care enough about me that they want me to make good choices. And please help me to make better choices in the future! In Your name, amen.

There is no joy while we are being punished. It is hard to take, but later we can see that good came from it. And it gives us the peace of being right with God.
HEBREWS 12:11 NLV

Day 130
LIGHT AND LIFE

Lord, will You use me to be a light in a very dark place? Please transform my life to be all that You want it to be. Help me to follow Your will for my life without grumbling and complaining. There are certain things I know I must do as part of growing up: go to school, do chores, be responsible, help my family. Sometimes I don't like all the responsibilities I have, but help me to carry them out with love and light in my heart. Help me to hold fast to Your Words, Lord. When so many around me are living in the dark, let me be light to them. Amen.

Do all things without grumbling or disputing, that you may be blameless and innocent, children of God without blemish in the midst of a crooked and twisted generation, among whom you shine as lights in the world, holding fast to the word of life.
PHILIPPIANS 2:14–16 ESV

Day 131
ANXIETY

God, whenever I'm worrying about things that are beyond my control, help me to remember Your words: "Do not be anxious about anything." I need to tell myself that in every situation. You are present, and You are looking out for me. You have provided for every living thing on the earth, so why should I doubt that You will take care of me? Help me to entrust my anxiety to You, to not take on the cares of tomorrow, and to lift everything up to You in prayer. You will never leave me or forsake me, and that assurance should remind me not to worry. Amen.

Do not be anxious about anything,
but in every situation, by prayer and petition,
with thanksgiving, present your requests to God.
PHILIPPIANS 4:6 NIV

Day 132

TROUBLE EVERYWHERE

Lord, sometimes it seems like everything that could go wrong does go wrong. I feel like troubles are falling on me from every side, and there's nothing I can do about it. But I know You're with me, Lord. No matter what happens, at least I don't have to face it alone. At least I know that as I deal with hard things, You're right beside me, holding my hand and giving me wisdom to get through them. Thank You, Lord, for loving me enough to stay with me even when things are hard. Thank You for giving me the wisdom to get through even the most difficult situations. Amen.

The righteous person may have many troubles,
but the LORD delivers him from them all.

PSALM 34:19 NIV

Day 133
CAN'T TAKE IT BACK

I'm learning, God, that my words can be helpful or hurtful. It's very easy to make another person feel bad by saying something unkind. I want to be in control of what I say even when I'm upset. I know that a fruit of the Spirit is self-control, and I sure do need it. Help me not to be used by Satan to hurt others, but instead, let me encourage them and make them feel loved and happy.

Thank You for forgiving me; I'm trusting You to help me remember this so I will be more careful next time. In Christ's name, amen.

Too much talk leads to sin.
Be sensible and keep your mouth shut.
PROVERBS 10:19 NLT

Day 134
PRAYER

Heavenly Father, You are the best listener in my life! Yet so often I forget to take advantage of Your listening ear. Thank You for providing me with people in my life who I can talk to about things, but help me to remember that You want to hear about things too. And I forget that prayer can be a conversation. I need to listen for You; You may not say anything, but You do make Yourself heard in my life. I can talk to You anywhere, anytime. Thank You for Your constantly listening ear and for all the ways that You encourage me and are patient with me. Amen.

Each morning you listen to my prayer, as I bring my requests to you and wait for your reply.
PSALM 5:3 CEV

Day 135

MY THOUGHTS

I want to be a "glass half full" type of girl, Lord. Sometimes I view it as half empty, don't I? I need Your help to control my thoughts. Help me to take every thought captive to Jesus as Your Word encourages me to do. Protect my mind and train me to dwell on the positive, the lovely, the blessings in my life. Help me to trust in Your truths rather than fall for the evil one's lies. I want to think on excellent, noble things. I want to walk in right paths and not become entangled in wrong ones that will lead me to destruction. Be the Lord of my thought life, I ask You today. Amen.

Finally, brothers and sisters, whatever is true, whatever is noble, whatever is right, whatever is pure, whatever is lovely, whatever is admirable—if anything is excellent or praiseworthy—think about such things.
PHILIPPIANS 4:8 NIV

Day 136
STANDING UP FOR OTHERS

I hear it every day—people talking about other people, Father. While I try not to gossip about others, sometimes I find myself in that awkward place of being around people who do, and I wonder exactly how to handle that. So, what do I do, Lord? Give me the words to speak in those situations. I want to honor You and honor others. I want to think the best of people. And I don't want to spread rumors! Even if something is true, that doesn't mean it needs to be shared. Help me encourage the people I'm around not to talk negatively but to speak the truth in love. Amen.

Who may worship in your sanctuary, LORD? Who may enter your presence on your holy hill? Those who lead blameless lives and do what is right, speaking the truth from sincere hearts. Those who refuse to gossip or harm their neighbors or speak evil of their friends.
PSALM 15:1–3 NLT

Day 137
LOVE OR BEAR A GRUDGE?

Father God, when someone does something to hurt me, I get angry and hold a grudge. I know that in life some people are mean-spirited. Yet how I respond to them is what counts. Lord, I can't love someone like that without Your power and strength. In fact, I don't even *want* to love them. I want them to feel as bad as they have made me feel. Please change my heart so that I can see them as You do. Help me to learn from Your example and not seek revenge or harbor bad feelings; rather, empower me to pray for those who have hurt me—and yes, to love them with Your love. Amen.

"Do not seek revenge or bear a grudge against anyone among your people, but love your neighbor as yourself."
LEVITICUS 19:18 NIV

Day 138
LOVING MY ENEMIES

I don't know if I have many enemies, Lord. But I do know there are a lot of people who don't like that I'm a Christian. They don't believe in You, and they are looking for any chance they can to dispute Your existence and make me feel stupid for believing. Help me to love them anyway. And help me to do good to them in any way that I can so that they might second-guess their thoughts about You. Let them see little glimpses of Your power and love through me.

Help me to be strong in You and in Your mighty power. Use me to bring light and love into the darkness. Amen.

"Love your enemies! Do good to them. Lend to them without expecting to be repaid. Then your reward from heaven will be very great, and you will truly be acting as children of the Most High, for he is kind to those who are unthankful and wicked."

LUKE 6:35 NLT

Day 139
JOY VS. HAPPINESS

Father, help me to remember the difference between happiness and joy. At times I think the words mean the same thing, but they really don't. Happiness is a result of what happens to and around me. But joy—*true* joy—comes from knowing that You love me so much and care about what happens to me. So even on the absolute worst of days, I can still have joy in my heart because I have You in and with me. I want to live a life full of joy, Jesus, and want others to see that I'm different. Because even when bad things happen, I can still have a spirit of joy and rest in Your goodness. Amen.

And so my heart is glad. My soul is full of joy.
My body also will rest without fear.
PSALM 16:9 NLV

Day 140
THE BEST BOOK OF ALL

Reading a good book is so satisfying, Lord. I love adventure stories, where the hero saves the day. I also like historical stories, set before I was born, because they help me know what life was like back then. I especially like to read books about people who've been through struggles, because I learn from what they've been through. It helps me know I'm not the only one who goes through stuff. Yes, a great book can totally lift my spirits! Thank You, Father, for the best book of all—one loaded with more adventure, more history, and more personal stories than any other. Your Word—the Bible—is action-packed! Amen.

"This book of the Law must not leave your mouth.
Think about it day and night, so you may be careful
to do all that is written in it. Then all will go well
with you. You will receive many good things."
JOSHUA 1:8 NLV

TELLING THE TRUTH

Lord, I don't like to think of myself as a liar, but sometimes it's easy to stretch the truth a little or tell just a teensy lie to make myself look better or to keep from getting in trouble. But when I tell one lie, I often must tell another to cover the first one. Then another and another. And before long, I don't know how to get out. I know You value honesty. I don't want to get in the habit of saying things that aren't true, even if they don't seem that important. Help me to speak the truth today and every day. Amen.

An honest answer is like a kiss on the lips.
PROVERBS 24:26 NIV

Day 142
KNOWLEDGE IS COOL

Heavenly Father, I wonder if Jesus went to school when He was a boy. The Bible doesn't tell us, but He probably did. Wow, wouldn't that be scary for the teacher if he had known that he was teaching the Son of God? Even though school isn't always much fun for me, I know it's good for me to learn. Thank You for giving me a mind that can understand and for all the help You give me as I open my books and study. You're an awesome tutor! Amen.

The fear of the LORD is the beginning of knowledge,
but fools despise wisdom and instruction.

PROVERBS 1:7 NIV

Day 143
MY BEST FOR YOU

God, slackers get on my nerves. Sometimes I need to remember that whole slacker thing for myself. I mean, I know You gave me special gifts and abilities, but that doesn't mean I should do less than my best just because certain things are beyond my comfort zone, right? Father, please help me to remember that every opportunity I have comes from You. And You expect me to give my all in *everything* I do. Please bring to mind every area in which I'm tempted to slack off—and keep me accountable, Lord, so I tamp down all temptation to give less than 100 percent. Thanks, God! I know You won't let me down! Amen.

Don't you realize that in a race everyone runs,
but only one person gets the prize? So run to win!
1 CORINTHIANS 9:24 NLT

Day 144
BEHIND THE SCENES

Lord, when I read Your Word, I see the amazing stories of all You have done for us on earth. Deep down, I know that Your Word is truth. It is there where I discover Your power to heal, move mountains, shake the world, strengthen the weak, and feed the hungry. There is nothing You cannot do! And there is nothing *I* cannot do if I have faith. You are often working behind the scenes. Every day I feel blessed for what You have given me—friends, family, food, fun. Right now I feel Your presence within me and all around me. And it is here, in You, that I have victory! Amen.

"If you embrace this kingdom life and don't doubt God, you'll. . .triumph over huge obstacles. This mountain, for instance, you'll tell, 'Go jump in the lake,' and it will jump. Absolutely everything, ranging from small to large, as you make it a part of your believing prayer, gets included as you lay hold of God."
MATTHEW 21:21–22 MSG

THE INSIDE RATHER THAN THE OUTSIDE

God, David was the youngest of Jesse's sons, and yet You chose him over the older and bigger ones. You saw something in young David's heart, didn't You, Lord? You selected him as king! I can relate to David, Father, the shepherd boy whom Jesse had not even bothered to call in from the field. No one imagined David would be the one chosen. No one ever seems to notice me either. I just feel really *average* sometimes, like there is nothing outstanding about me. The story of David is a great reminder, Lord, that You use regular people—sometimes even those whom no one would suspect—to do special things in Your kingdom! Amen.

"The Lord does not look at the things people look at. People look at the outward appearance, but the Lord looks at the heart."
1 Samuel 16:7 niv

Day 146
LONELINESS

Heavenly Father, in Philippians 4:19, Your Word tells me that You will supply everything I need. And in Matthew 6:32 and Luke 12:30, it says that You know exactly what I need and will provide it for me. Why is that so hard to grasp? I guess that's where faith and trust come in. Lord, help me to keep my focus on You and to believe the truth found in Your Word and not rely on my emotions or feelings. There *are* people in my life who love me and care about me. You have placed them there because You care for me most of all. When loneliness or circumstances overwhelm me, remind me of Your love for me. Amen.

When I am overwhelmed, you alone know the way I should turn.
PSALM 142:3 NLT

Day 147
CAN'T DECIDE?

Lord, every morning I rush to get ready for school. Running out the door, I wonder if I'll have a good or bad day. I fear that I'll do something stupid or embarrassing. The truth is that I don't need to worry about those things or make any decisions on my own. You, my God, greet me each morning with Your love. If I take a few minutes in the morning to pray, You help me through whatever I might have to face and any decisions I need to make. Help me today, Father. Let Your love guide my path in whatever decisions I face. Show me the way. Amen.

---

*Remind me each morning of your constant
love, for I put my trust in you. My prayers go
up to you; show me the way I should go.*
Psalm 143:8 GNT

Day 148
A WORK IN PROGRESS

I mess up a lot, God. I try to live as Your Word instructs, but I find myself giving in to temptations at times. Then I have to find my way back to You again. You are always there, ready to take me back. Just like a sculptor transforms a lump of clay into something extraordinary, You are steadily molding me into the woman I will become. And even then, I will be imperfect. You will always be teaching me and guiding me until Jesus comes back. Thank You, Father. You have begun something great in me, and I am a wonderful work in progress. I love You, Lord. Amen.

And I am certain that God, who began the good work within you, will continue his work until it is finally finished on the day when Christ Jesus returns.
PHILIPPIANS 1:6 NLT

Day 149
MOUTH GUARD

I should have control of my tongue, Jesus, but I don't always think about my words before they pop out of my mouth. But You know that because You hear everything I say—the good *and* the bad. Please forgive me for the times I say things I shouldn't. You made my tongue, heavenly Father, but You made it to honor You and those You have created. Please help me to think about what I say before I say it and to choose only words that will be pure, positive, and encouraging to everyone around me. Amen.

Set a guard, O Lord, over my mouth;
keep watch over the door of my lips!
PSALM 141:3 ESV

Day 150
WHAT A MESS!

I'll admit it, Lord. . .sometimes I can be a little messy. My space gets cluttered. Dirty clothes cover the floor. I can't always find my school supplies or my device chargers when I need them. I'm not thrilled when my parents ask me to clean up. Seems pointless. After all, it will just get messy again! So I don't always do the best job, to be honest. But if cleanliness matters to You, God—and it does—it should matter to me too. Help me to do the very best with the things that have been given to me. I know this brings honor to You! Amen.

"Then I will put clean water on you, and you will be clean.
I will make you clean from all your unclean ways."
EZEKIEL 36:25 NLV

Day 151
COMFORT FROM GOD

Heavenly Father, sometimes I find it hard to feel comforted by You because You can't physically give me a hug and I haven't heard the actual sound of Your voice. Help me to feel Your presence in my heart, even if I can't see You with my eyes. I want to be comforted by Your Word and through prayer. Remind me of these things when I'm feeling lonely or depressed. I know that all comfort and all love come from You. I just forget sometimes. Help me to always remember Your love and Your comfort that is in my heart. Amen.

Show me a sign of your goodness.
When my enemies look, they will be ashamed.
You, LORD, have helped me and comforted me.
PSALM 86:17 NCV

Day 152

THE UPS AND DOWNS
OF FRIENDSHIP

Thank You for my many friends, Father. Some I've had for a long time, and other friendships have developed more recently. There are those I hang out with and others I trust with my deepest secrets and dreams. I ask for wisdom in choosing my friends. I ask that You guide me to the ones who will be a good influence and will encourage me in my walk with You. Thank You for being the most perfect friend anyone could ever have. You're never too busy to listen, and You will always make decisions based on what is best for me, whether I like it or not. There is no better friend than You! Amen.

---

*Friends come and friends go, but a true
friend sticks by you like family.*
PROVERBS 18:24 MSG

Day 153
IMPERFECTION AND AIRBRUSHING

Heavenly Father, my face is a mess today. And here I am in front of the mirror again hoping that I'll see a miracle take place—and suddenly the pimples will be gone, leaving beautiful, clear skin in their place. But I know that's not going to happen. So, I have to just make the best of it. Thank You that someone invented spot treatments and all those other special soaps and lotions. At least I live in a century where there is some help! So, today I'll cover what I can and then ask You to shine through me because that's what matters most anyway. Amen.

I will praise the Lord at all times.
PSALM 34:1 NLT

Day 154

THE PRESENT MOMENT

Sometimes, Father, I want to be fully grown up. I want to make decisions on my own, do what I want to do, when I want to do it. Then at other times, I'm so glad I'm still a teen. Help me to be happy in the present moment, Lord. To live for today and not worry about tomorrow. Remind me that every day with You is a good day. And so, I will be content, learning from others and waiting for You to grow me up into the person You have planned me to be. Thank You, Lord, for being with me every stage of my life, gently leading me, tenderly supporting me, and blessing me day after day. Amen.

This is the day the LORD has made;
we will rejoice and be glad in it.
PSALM 118:24 NKJV

Day 155
GOD HOLDS ME UP

What a wonderful promise I have in Your Word that You are my God! You tell me that You are with me and that I don't ever need to be afraid or worried. You promise to help, to give me strength, and to hold me up. Does it get any better than that? Thank You, Lord, that because of my faith in Jesus, I am Your daughter. I am a treasured daughter of the King of kings, loved and protected by none other than You! I pray that all the days of my life I will remember that I am never alone. I always have You, my God. Amen.

"Do not fear, for I am with you; do not be afraid, for I am your God. I will strengthen you, I will also help you, I will also uphold you with My righteous right hand."

ISAIAH 41:10 NASB

Day 156
ENDURANCE

Some days just aren't that great. Life gets hard, and I get tired. But the last thing I want to do is give up. God, I need Your help in going forward. The dictionary defines *endurance* as "the ability to withstand hardship or adversity." I don't want to be beaten down by life or the things that happen to me. I want to be the best I can be, to win the prize, to reach the goal. This verse in Hebrews tells me I can do that by keeping my eyes on Jesus. He endured so much for me. God, help me look to Jesus as my example. Give me the strength I need to continue. Amen.

Let us strip off every weight that slows us down, especially the sin that so easily trips us up. And let us run with endurance the race God has set before us. We do this by keeping our eyes on Jesus, the champion who initiates and perfects our faith. Because of the joy awaiting him, he endured the cross, disregarding its shame. Now he is seated in the place of honor beside God's throne.

HEBREWS 12:1–2 NLT

Day 157
A GIVING HEART

Dear God, I have a desire to be genuinely kind to people. Not just my family and friends—*everyone*! The cashier at my favorite ice cream shop, the librarian at school, and even peers I don't know well. Some people are much easier to love than others, and when it's hard to love someone, I need You to show me how. I want kindness to be something that I am known for, especially with my friends when they are going through a hard time and need a listening ear. Please help my thoughts, words, and actions reflect kindness and love to everyone that I meet, and help me to be kind and loyal to my friends. Amen.

Never let loyalty and kindness leave you! Tie them around your neck as a reminder. Write them deep within your heart.

PROVERBS 3:3 NLT

Day 158
WORRY

Sometimes my thoughts swirl faster than my mind can keep up with. I think about the future and all the what-ifs, what I hope will happen, and what might not. I look at every angle of a problem that could happen, wanting to be prepared "just in case." When I struggle with wanting and not having or wondering if something will or won't happen, I need to get off the spinning merry-go-round of emotion and trust You, God, to give me what I need. Jesus says that You will meet our human concerns. I don't want to worry myself into missing what I have, Lord. Help me to trust in You for everything I need. Amen.

Give your burdens to the LORD, and he will take care of you. He will not permit the godly to slip and fall.
PSALM 55:22 NLT

Day 159

WHAT IS MY PURPOSE?

God, I know from Your Word that You have a plan for everyone who loves You. . .and because I love You, I guess that includes me. But I don't know what Your plans are. It would be great if You'd just write them on my ceiling, but then I wouldn't have to trust You as much. And I do want to learn to trust You more. Show me ways I can use my talents for You, Father. And please help me to be patient as I try to figure out my purpose. In the meantime, I will continue following You, trusting You every step of the way.

---

*For we are his workmanship, created in Christ
Jesus for good works, which God prepared
beforehand, that we should walk in them.*
EPHESIANS 2:10 ESV

Day 160
RESTING IN YOU

Heavenly Father, Your Word says that I should stop, that taking a rest—a break—is a good idea. Even You took a break when You were creating the world, Father! I need to learn from You! If resting was important to You, it should be important to me too. Do I need to take a break from any activities in my life? If so, show me which ones! In the meantime, I pray that You will give me energy to get through the things I must do. The Bible says that You will give strength to those who are tired. I get really tired sometimes, so I could use a double dose of Your strength! Amen.

He gives strength to the weary and increases the power of the weak. Even youths grow tired and weary, and young men stumble and fall; but those who hope in the LORD will renew their strength.
ISAIAH 40:29–31 NIV

Day 161
CHOOSING JOY

Dear Lord, whenever I'm down or going through a hard time, give me joy. I know that I often focus much more on being happy, but I should focus more on joy because it has a lasting effect. I think that finding joy means focusing on the little blessings that You give me every day, like a beautiful sunset, or time with friends, or making someone else smile. Help me always choose joy and to spread joy to the lives of those around me. Happy times make it easier to go through difficult times, and for that I am very thankful. Amen.

You make known to me the path of life; you will fill me with joy in your presence, with eternal pleasures at your right hand.

PSALM 16:11 NIV

Day 162
HEALING WORDS

Why can't I control my mouth, Lord? No matter how hard I try, I keep messing up. The words just spill out before I realize what I'm saying. I need to learn to think before I speak and choose my words more carefully. I want to build people up, not tear them down. I want to be the kind of person whose words bring healing and hope, not heartache and hurt. Help me to edit my words while they're still in my head, before they come out of my mouth. I want to honor You and share Your love, Lord, with everything I say. Amen.

The words of the reckless pierce like swords,
but the tongue of the wise brings healing.
PROVERBS 12:18 NIV

Day 163
HAPPY IN HOPING

Lord, when I was little, it didn't take much to make me happy—a new toy or book or a trip to McDonald's. But now I know that life isn't always fixed easily—there aren't any Band-Aids for divorce or cancer or friends who move away. Life can really hurt! But no matter how bad things get, I know there is always hope because You promise You'll never leave me and that someday I'll live with You. Sometimes I overhear others talking about the bad things happening in their lives, and they seem to have no hope at all. Help me to share with them the solid hope I have because of You, Jesus! Amen.

Blessed are those whose help is the God of Jacob,
whose hope is in the LORD their God.
PSALM 146:5 NIV

Day 164
SEEN BUT NOT HEARD

Help me, Lord, to be an example to others! Give me the patience to think before I speak. And then give me the right words to say—or not say—at the right time. Give me the heart to love everyone, to be gentle, kind, and respectful. Boost my faith so that I can have confidence in myself and, even more importantly, in You. Help me to stay pure in thought, word, and deed. I am trusting You, Lord, to set me on the right path in all situations. I am counting on You to eventually make me into the woman You know I can be. Amen.

Don't let anyone put you down because you're young. Teach believers with your life: by word, by demeanor, by love, by faith, by integrity. Stay at your post reading Scripture, giving counsel, teaching.
1 TIMOTHY 4:12 MSG

Day 165
A CHOICE TO MAKE

Father, I know that I have a choice to make. It seems like I am faced with it every single day. I must choose whether to follow the world or to travel the narrow road with You. I know that Your guidelines for my life are set with my best interests in mind. You are not trying to keep me from anything that is good. Every perfect gift comes from You, my heavenly Father. When You look at my heart, I pray that You are pleased. I will always choose You over this world. Give me the strength, wisdom, and endurance I will need as I continue to walk with You. Amen.

He said to them, "You are the ones who justify yourselves
in the eyes of others, but God knows your hearts.
What people value highly is detestable in God's sight."
LUKE 16:15 NIV

GIVING TILL IT HURTS

Heavenly Father, Jesus' words in Luke chapter 6 say that the measure I use to give to others will be the same measure used to give to me. That's a pretty good return! The funny part is, even though it may be painful at first to give up something that I want for myself and give it to others, in the end I get more benefit than they do! God, help me to continue to think of others before myself and to be willing to give without hesitation. I will trust You to bring back to me all I need in the same way I have given to others. Amen.

---

*"Give, and you will receive. You will be given much.
Pressed down, shaken together, and running
over, it will spill into your lap. The way you give
to others is the way God will give to you."*
LUKE 6:38 NCV

Day 167
JUST ASK

Jesus, You said that when I ask, I'll receive. I know that doesn't mean You'll always say yes; rather, You *will answer* my prayers. Help me to seek You more through prayer. I believe that You never turn from anyone who comes to You with an open, sincere heart. I open my heart to You now, Lord. I seek Your will for my life and ask that You give me wisdom, strength, direction, and guidance. Thank You for listening to my prayers and answering! Even when the answer is "no" or "we'll see." Amen.

"Ask, and you will receive; seek, and you will find;
knock, and the door will be opened to you."
MATTHEW 7:7 GNT

Day 168
TALKING KINDLY

Dear God, it seems so easy to get caught up in talking about other people behind their backs. So many of my friends do it, and it's hard not to join in sometimes. Please forgive me for being a part of that and help me to change. Please give me fresh ideas and topics to talk about with my friends, so I don't get sucked into talking about other people in negative ways. I want the words of my mouth to be pleasing to you, Father (Psalm 19:14). Help me to choose good friends who talk kindly about others. Help me not to be naive either. If my friends talk about other people behind their back, they are probably talking about me too. Amen.

It is foolish to belittle one's neighbor;
a sensible person keeps quiet. A gossip goes
around telling secrets, but those who are
trustworthy can keep a confidence.
PROVERBS 11:12–13 NLT

Day 169

WONDERFULLY MADE

Your Word tells me that I am wonderfully made. I want to remember that, Lord, when the world tells me differently. I know that being healthy and caring for my physical body is important, but sometimes I feel like I am on a treadmill going nowhere. I don't want to be dissatisfied with who I am. There are times when I need a new perspective. I am thankful that when I look at myself through Your eyes, I see a different kind of person than what the world might see. Help me to *like* who I am, God, and to remember that I am *me*—the me You made me to be! Amen.

---

*You made all the delicate, inner parts of my
body and knit me together in my mother's womb.
Thank you for making me so wonderfully complex!
Your workmanship is marvelous—how well I know it.*
PSALM 139:13–14 NLT

A VOLCANO OF ANGER

Temper, temper! Father, sometimes I let mine get the best of me. I feel like a volcano is stirring up inside of me and then. . . *bam!* I blow! You tell me in Your Word that I shouldn't let my anger reach the boiling point. I should be quick to listen and slow to speak. And when I do speak, my words shouldn't be angry or demanding! Getting in arguments isn't a good thing. Blowing up at people isn't either. You want me to be kind to everyone. So, I ask You to remove my temper today. Calm me down and show me how to react the way You would react. I trust You, Lord. Amen.

A servant of the Lord must not quarrel but must be kind to everyone, be able to teach, and be patient with difficult people.
2 Timothy 2:24 nlt

Day 171
HONEST WORDS

Lord, when I'm tempted to lie to get out of trouble or to be polite, remind me how honesty is important. I want my family and friends to be able to trust what I say; I want to be known for honesty in every area of my life. I know that You will never judge me for the thoughts or feelings that I have, but I sometimes judge myself or lie to myself about things. Give me the grace to be honest with myself and others when I've messed up and done something wrong. Amen.

If you do the right thing, honesty will be your guide. But if you are crooked, you will be trapped by your own dishonesty.
PROVERBS 11:3 CEV

Day 172
LET SOMEBODY ELSE

I'm good at a lot of things, Lord. The problem is, not everyone knows it. And when I tell people about all my great gifts, no one seems impressed. That's when I realize. . .I was bragging. I don't want to come across as a brag. Help me remember that no matter how hard it is to feel passed over and ignored, it's usually best to stay quiet about my own strengths. I should do my best in everything and let others figure out what I'm good at. Praise always feels better when it comes from someone else and not from my own mouth. Remind me of that today, Lord. Amen.

Let someone else praise you, and not your own mouth; an outsider, and not your own lips.
PROVERBS 27:2 NIV

Day 173
GUILTY FEELINGS

God, I feel guilty today. I've done something that is wrong, and I feel terribly dirty inside. I know I shouldn't have done it, but I did it anyway. Now I am sorry, but I can't get rid of this feeling that I'm in the shadows and there's no way out. I know that You are a God of mercy and forgiveness, so I'm coming to You right now and asking You to make me clean. Please forgive me and restore me in Your sight. I'm glad that Jesus died for my sins and that You are ready to forgive when I ask. Thank You for loving me always. In Jesus' name, amen.

If we confess our sins, He is faithful and just to forgive us our sins and to cleanse us from all unrighteousness.
1 JOHN 1:9 NKJV

Day 174

ALL THAT REALLY MATTERS

Lord, please show me how I can serve You, how I can show Your love to everyone I meet, how I can follow Your commandment to love You with all my heart, soul, and mind, and to love others as I love myself. When I really think about it, loving You and others is all that matters in this world. Yet sometimes it's not easy. So, I really need Your strength every moment of the day. Give me the peace that comes from following You. And help me to encourage others as You encourage me. In Jesus' name I pray, amen.

Some people have given up the habit of meeting for worship, but we must not do that. We should keep on encouraging each other, especially since you know that the day of the Lord's coming is getting closer.
HEBREWS 10:25 CEV

LIGHT IN THE DARKNESS

I remember as a little girl being so afraid of the dark. There was just something frightening about not being able to see in the darkness! I have to admit, Father, the darkness still scares me. Not literal darkness. . .but the darkness of the world. Help me, Lord, when I am in the midst of evil, to remember what You have taught me in the light. You are always with me, and I can always call on You to shine Your light into the darkness and show me the way to go. I trust You, Lord. Lead me through this dark world on a path filled with Your glorious light. Amen.

If I say, "Surely the darkness will hide me and the light become night around me," even the darkness will not be dark to you; the night will shine like the day, for darkness is as light to you.
PSALM 139:11–12 NIV

Day 176
THOUGHTS ABOUT SCIENCE CLASS

Father, we're talking about the *E* word in school right now. *Evolution*—the origin of the earth and humankind and the development of the species. Some of it sounds convincing, but I believe what the Bible says: You created the world and everything in it. I'm glad, God, for all those Sunday school lessons about creation. I know You created the world—and *me*—with a purpose. I know I won't convince all my friends that Creation is the right view, but help me stick to the truth when I am asked. I don't want to cave in because I'm afraid to be different or ridiculed. Amen.

For in six days the LORD made the heavens and the earth, the sea, and all that is in them.
EXODUS 20:11 NKJV

Day 177
THANK YOU
FOR LOVING ME

It's hard for me to realize that You love me even when I don't deserve it, Father. You are perfect in every way, and I am so imperfect! Thank You that no matter how unlovable I am on certain days, You still keep on loving me! When I feel so unlovable and undeserving, You remind me that Your love extends far beyond what I could ever imagine. That's amazing! I'm so blessed because even when I deserve Your anger, You keep on loving me. You accept me as I am; You forgive my sins and cleanse my heart. I love You, Lord. Thank You for loving me so much. Amen.

God is sheer mercy and grace; not easily angered, he's rich in love. He doesn't endlessly nag and scold, nor hold grudges forever. He doesn't treat us as our sins deserve, nor pay us back in full for our wrongs. As high as heaven is over the earth, so strong is his love to those who fear him.
PSALM 103:8–10 MSG

Day 178
CHOOSE LIFE

I choose life, Lord. Your Word tells me that eternal life is knowing You through Your Son, Jesus Christ (John 17:3) and that You came to give me abundant life (John 10:10)—even here, right now on this earth, as I wait to be with You forever in heaven. Help me to remember this on hard days. Please stay close to my heart always. Let my life be a reminder to everyone around me that You are alive and well and still working in the hearts and minds of those who seek after You. Thank You for giving me life, Jesus. I praise Your name! Amen.

I am offering you life or death, blessings or curses.
Now, choose life! Then you and your children
may live. To choose life is to love the LORD your
God, obey him, and stay close to him.
DEUTERONOMY 30:19–20 NCV

Day 179
FORGIVE THEM?

Dear Jesus, my friend just hurt me, and the pain feels like it's more than I can handle. I wish You knew what it felt like. . .then You'd understand. Oh. . .but You *do* understand what it's like. Your friend took a bribe to turn You in when You hadn't done anything wrong. You were humiliated. You were mocked and tortured. And You were killed in a cruel way. But some of Your last words were ones of forgiveness. And Jesus, I have hurt You with my sin, but You keep forgiving *me* anyway. Please give me the strength to be like You. Help me to forgive whether I receive an apology or not. In Your precious name, amen.

Be kind to one another, tenderhearted,
forgiving one another, as God in Christ forgave you.
EPHESIANS 4:32 ESV

Day 180
SELF-DISCIPLINE

Lord, I admit, it's not always easy to do everything I'm told. But the Bible says that You can give me self-discipline. This means I shouldn't have to wait on others to remind me to do things like clean my room, put dishes away, or do my homework. With Your help, Father, I can do those things on my own, without being reminded repeatedly. Please teach me how to be self-disciplined, Lord. Can You remind me to take care of things and show me how to be responsible? I want to mature to be the very best me I can possibly be! With Your help, I know I can do it! Amen.

For the Spirit God gave us does not make us timid,
but gives us power, love and self-discipline.
2 TIMOTHY 1:7 NIV

Day 181
WHEN I FEEL INSECURE

Heavenly Father, I feel so insecure sometimes. I don't want to feel this way, and I don't always know what to do when this happens. Whenever I'm feeling insecure, help me to remember to turn to You for the security that I need. Help me find my identity in You—not in the things I do, how I look, or whom I hang out with. I know that I am Your child; remind me of that when I feel like no one loves me or wants to be around me. Thank You for Your constant love and security, heavenly Father. Amen.

Only God can save me, and I calmly wait for him. God alone is the mighty rock that keeps me safe and the fortress where I am secure.
PSALM 62:1–2 CEV

Day 182

AVOID GOSSIP

I don't want to be a gossip, Lord. I've been hurt by gossip, and I don't want my words to hurt other people. I want to be accepted. I want to be part of the group. A lot of times the best way to be part of the group is to join in their mean talk. Many times, I find myself sharing personal things about my own life with these mean-spirited people in hopes that they'll accept me as one of them. Help me to be kind in my words about others and wise in what I share about myself. And help me find friends who want to be kind and wise too. Amen.

A gossip betrays a confidence;
so avoid anyone who talks too much.
PROVERBS 20:19 NIV

Day 183
CROWNING GLORY
. . .OR NOT!

My hair doesn't like to cooperate with me, Lord. When I'm getting ready to go somewhere, it just refuses to look like I want it to. I hope other people don't think my hair looks as bad as I think it does. But thank You, God, that You don't love me for my hair. You saw me before I was born when I didn't have any hair at all—and You've loved me from the beginning of time. So please help me to do the best I can and believe that I will get better with practice. I'll probably still have bad hair days occasionally, but I don't have to judge my life by them. Amen.

But the very hairs of your head are all numbered.
MATTHEW 10:30 KJV

Day 184

IN GOD'S GRIP

Father God, many days my courage and my strength are tested. I'm wondering if I'm making the right decisions. That's when fear and confusion begin to creep in. Then, just when I feel myself beginning to panic, I remember that not only are You *with* me in every situation I face, but You are also going *before* me, clearing the way. Help me walk *Your* way with the courage You provide twenty-four hours a day. Keep reminding me that You will never let me down but will raise me up to face any challenges that come my way. Thank You for keeping me in Your grip.

---

*"Be strong. Take courage. Don't be intimidated. Don't give them a second thought because G*OD*, your God, is striding ahead of you. He's right there with you. He won't let you down; he won't leave you."*
DEUTERONOMY 31:6 MSG

Day 185
HUMILITY

Help me to remember that none of my goals can be met on my own, Father. I need Your help. And when I am in leadership roles or win an award of any kind, I want to always remember to give You the glory. I will serve as a leader at my school or church or in any situation You see fit. But even if I rise to the top, let me always remember You are above me. I am Your humble servant. Use me as You will. And give me opportunities to build others up. I don't want to be jealous if someone outshines me. Envy is never a good feeling! Help me to always choose humility. Amen.

Whoever is the greatest should be the servant of the others. If you put yourself above others, you will be put down. But if you humble yourself, you will be honored.
MATTHEW 23:11–12 CEV

Day 186
WORDS CAN HURT YOU

God, please help me guard my mouth so that I never hurt others as I have been hurt by thoughtless words. Let my words encourage others and not tear them down. Even in joking around, words can hurt. I don't like to be teased about certain things, and it's not always easy to know what might bother others. I like making others laugh, but it should never be at another person's expense. Help me be kind to others, and when they are unkind to me, help me forgive them. Help me respond to those around me in a way that is honoring to them—and to You, God. Amen.

Just as damaging as a madman shooting a deadly weapon is someone who lies to a friend and then says, "I was only joking."
PROVERBS 26:18–19 NLT

Day 187
WHY WORRY? PRAY!

Father, I worry about a lot of things. Each day gives me something new to worry about! I just can't seem to help myself. Yet You tell Your children not to worry but to pray instead. I need help with that, Lord. My first reaction is to fret rather than pray. I know You care about me and the things I care about. So, Father, I give You all my worries right now and ask that You help me sort through them. Please give me the answers I need and the peace that comes with surrendering my problems and concerns to You. Thank You, Lord. Amen.

Don't worry about anything; instead, pray about everything. Tell God what you need, and thank him for all he has done. Then you will experience God's peace.
PHILIPPIANS 4:6–7 NLT

Day 188

A MEASURE OF LOVE

Heavenly Father, I know You oppose the proud just like the Bible says in James 4:6. Your Word also tells me that You show favor to the humble. I certainly don't want You to be against me, Lord. I pray for Your favor on my life. Help me not to condemn and judge other people when I have no right to do that. But when a friend of mine is choosing sin over Your plan, help me be able to talk to her out of love and friendship. Give me wisdom to lovingly confront the friends that I feel You nudging me to talk to. But help me always do it with a clean heart before You. Amen.

"For in the same way you judge others, you will be judged, and with the measure you use, it will be measured to you."

MATTHEW 7:2 NIV

Day 189
LIVING WITHOUT REGRETS

Heavenly Father, I'm struggling with guilt from a bad choice. It feels like I'll need to carry it every day for the rest of my life. But Your Word tells me that if I say I'm sorry for my sin, You will take it away. And not only that, You choose to forget about it! Your promises are true—so if that's what You say, then I can believe it. Your Word also tells me that I don't have to do a lot of good things to make up for my sin. And so, Lord Jesus, I ask for Your forgiveness for what I've done. I thank You, Father! In Jesus' name, amen.

"For I will forgive their wickedness and will remember their sins no more."
HEBREWS 8:12 NIV

Day 190
WHAT'S HAPPENING TOMORROW?

Sometimes I wish I could see into the future, Lord! But I'll have to wait. One day I'll know Your plan for me; but in the meantime, please help me with all of the changes I'm going through—in my body, my mind, and my heart. It seems like every day I'm changing a little more. Guess that's part of maturing. Everyone goes through changes, so I know I'm not the only one. And I'm sure everyone gets a little scared about the future. Remind me that You've got this, Lord! You will direct my path and will give me wisdom as I go through changes, big and small! Amen.

Trust in the LORD with all your heart and lean not on your own understanding; in all your ways submit to him, and he will make your paths straight.
PROVERBS 3:5–6 NIV

Day 191
NOT THE POPULAR THING

God, sometimes I find myself changing my interests or who I hang out with based on what other people think. I know that changing who I am isn't a good way to be happy and content. When I'm in a situation where I feel pressure to do things because they are "cool," help me to stop and think about what I'm doing and not give in to the pressure of my peers. Help me to stand up for what I believe and show others that I believe in You and want to glorify You with my words and actions. The main goal in my life shouldn't be popularity, and sometimes I forget that. Please remind me of this. Amen.

So with God and Christ as witnesses, I command
you to preach God's message. Do it willingly,
even if it isn't the popular thing to do.
2 TIMOTHY 4:1–2 CEV

Day 192
QUIET TIME

Dear God, I really struggle to make time for You in my life. I want to set aside time daily to spend talking with You and reading Your Word. It is so easy for me to spend time with my friends or to do fun things, and when I'm in a rush or stressed, time with You is the first thing that I give up. Help me to be faithful in spending time with You regularly, building my relationship with You, and not just when I need Your help. Help me to remember that You are more than just a "fixer" and that I should talk to You about all the good things in my life too. Amen.

I thirst for the living God. When can I go to meet with him?
PSALM 42:2 NCV

Day 193
PRAYING FOR MY PRINCE

God, I want to get married someday to the man of my dreams. I know that not everyone gets married, but I hope it's in Your plan for me. I have a lot of things on my list that I'd like to have in a future husband, but I want You to have the final say. Today, I pray for the man who will someday be my husband. Give his parents wisdom to train him right; give him a pastor who will preach truth to him; and give him a heart that wants to follow You. Bring us together in Your timing and bless our lives together. In Jesus' name, amen.

For everything there is a season. . . . A time to love. . .
ECCLESIASTES 3:1, 8 NLT

Day 194

A PURPOSE AND A PLAN

Your Word says that You, Lord, are working out for my good everything that happens in my life. You have a plan for me. And there's a purpose to that plan. So, help me to let disappointment and discouragement roll off me like water off a duck's back. Help me to just shrug it off when things don't go my way. Help me to look on the bright side, seeing Your hand and Your heart in my life, knowing that, like my parents, You know and want what's best for me—You have a better way. Amen.

We are assured and know that [God being a partner in their labor] all things work together and are [fitting into a plan] for good to and for those who love God and are called according to [His] design and purpose.
ROMANS 8:28 AMPC

Day 195

AN EXAMPLE

I am just a teenager, God. There are many things I can't do—like staying out as late as I want! There are lots of things I can't control—such as where I live or even what I have for dinner. But You tell me in Your Word that I should be an example for other believers. Saying I am young is not an excuse. I have accepted You as my Savior, and that should show in how I talk and act. When others look at me, they should see that Jesus lives in my heart. They won't know that unless I love freely and choose to remain pure and faithful. Use me to do great things, Father, even while I am young! Amen.

Commit your way to the LORD;
trust in him, and he will act.
PSALM 37:5 ESV

Day 196
TELL THE TRUTH

Heavenly Father, I don't want to be left in the dark about things. I would much rather someone come to me and tell me what is going on, even if it is painful, so I think that is the best way for me to behave too. I know You honor truth, Lord. There's a verse in the Bible that talks about "speaking the truth in love" (Ephesians 4:15 NKJV). I think that means that we can be truthful, but at the same time, we can be kind to others. Help me to lovingly speak truth to others. Amen.

Gentle words are a tree of life; a deceitful
tongue crushes the spirit.
PROVERBS 15:4 NLT

Day 197
NO PRESSURE

Father, the Bible says that sin came into this world when Adam and Eve disobeyed You. The devil tempted and deceived Eve, and then she influenced Adam to disobey You too. It's not so different today. Help me to avoid peer pressure and temptations so that I stay obedient to Your will for my life. When I'm tempted to do something wrong, give me the strength to stay on track. Adam and Eve messed up, and sometimes I do too. But I'm grateful for Your forgiveness and the opportunity for another chance. Please help me to obey You and not accuse someone else for my failings. Amen.

The man replied, "It was the woman you gave me who gave me the fruit, and I ate it." Then the LORD God asked the woman, "What have you done?" "The serpent deceived me," she replied. "That's why I ate it."
GENESIS 3:12–13 NLT

Day 198
A GIFT OF PEACE

Jesus, You tell me not to be troubled or afraid and to accept Your gift of peace. . .and I want to do that more than anything. I don't know why I still let some problems get me down. I don't understand why I let myself get so scared and nervous about so many things! It shows my lack of faith, and I'm really sorry for that. Please help me to grow in my faith and trust in You. Thank You for Your amazing gifts. I know that no one else can fill me with peace in my mind and heart like You do. Let me accept those gifts and remember them always. Amen.

"I am leaving you with a gift—peace of mind and heart. And the peace I give is a gift the world cannot give. So don't be troubled or afraid."
JOHN 14:27 NLT

Day 199
LOVING OTHERS

Lord Jesus, I know You tell me to love everyone. That's easy to do when they're nice to me or don't hurt my feelings. But how can I do that when I don't even *like* some people? Help me to remember that I'm not always so loveable either, but I'm still loved. There is nothing I can do to make You stop loving me. Please give me a heart to love others like You do—not based on whether I think they deserve it or not, but rather just because they are creations You have made and You love, just like me. Amen.

"My command is this: Love each other as I have loved you."
JOHN 15:12 NIV

Day 200
THE RUMOR MILL

Sometimes I get caught up in gossip, Lord. Someone starts a rumor about someone else, and they tell me. Then I text the secret to a friend. . . . Gossip is like a forest fire! It spreads quickly and hurts a lot of people in the process. Can You help me put out the forest fire instead of spreading it, Father? When someone tells me some "juicy gossip," please close my mouth! And instead, remind me to pray for the person who's being gossiped about and to keep my heart pure. I want to be known as someone who brings people together, not someone who divides friends by gossiping. Amen.

Whoever covers an offense seeks love, but he who repeats a matter separates close friends.
PROVERBS 17:9 ESV

HARMFUL HUMOR

Lord, I was with some of my friends recently when they began teasing someone. At first, I thought it was funny. Then I found myself joining in. But something inside of me—it must've been Your Spirit—told me that the teasing was wrong. And I began feeling embarrassed for my friends and sorry for the person being mocked. Sadly, I didn't have the courage to tell my friends to stop. Instead, I just walked away. Help me to find the courage to help others who are being teased and to speak up when my friends are being unkind. Remind me that every person is special in Your eyes. Amen.

Whoever mocks poor people insults their Creator;
gloating over misfortune is a punishable crime.
PROVERBS 17:5 MSG

LOVE AND RESPECT

I hear all the time about how loving and kind You are, God. I hear about Your compassion and mercy. But I've also heard that I should fear You. I want to better understand what that means. Why should I fear You if You're good and kind? I love You, Lord. I also understand that You are God, and if I go against Your ways, You will discipline me. The reason You discipline me is because You love me and You want the best for me. Thank You for loving me that much. Help me to always have the right kind of respect for Your ways, Lord. Amen.

"These are the ones I look on with favor: those who are humble and contrite in spirit, and who tremble at my word."
ISAIAH 66:2 NIV

Day 203
DEPENDING ON GOD

So often I just jump into things without talking it over with You, Lord. I want to do better about that. I want us to become so close that I wouldn't think of making plans without You. Can we be a team? Will You lead me and walk alongside me? Be at the center of my thinking and guide me as I create goals for myself. Soon I will have even more decisions to make for my future beyond high school. To prepare myself, I want to get into the habit of walking with You. I commit my ways to You, Lord. Please bless me and allow my plans to succeed. I will give You all the glory. Amen.

Depend on the LORD in whatever you do,
and your plans will succeed.
PROVERBS 16:3 NCV

Day 204
BLESSED ALL OVER AGAIN

Lord, help me to realize that in a world where so many people have so little, I have so very much. Create in me a grateful spirit and a heart that cares to share. Show me what I might give away to bless others. I know that when I give of myself— whether it is a material thing or an act of service—all thoughts of lack disappear. I am overcome with love and joy because I'm following Your law to love You and to love others as I love myself. When I make it all about pleasing You—by giving from the bottom of my heart and closet—I find myself blessed all over again! Amen.

All must give as they are able, according to the
blessings given to them by the Lord your God.
DEUTERONOMY 16:17 NLT

TRUST IN THE LORD

Help me to realize, Father, that it will always be a tricky balance to determine which people in my life are trustworthy. But I can *always* trust You. You will never leave me or lead me down a wrong path. If I trust in You, You promise to direct me and to make Your plans clear to me as I journey through life. What a wonderful promise! Give me wisdom about which friends I can trust but help me to have an open heart and mind. I know that I need Christian friends in whom I can confide. Amen.

---

*Those who know the LORD trust him, because
he will not leave those who come to him.*

PSALM 9:10 NCV

Day 206
GOD UNDERSTANDS

Lord, I am so frustrated. No one understands me. I guess they try, but my parents are so out of touch with what I am feeling. My friends are too concerned with their own problems to care about mine. I want to believe that You understand me. I know You created me and that You love me. But do You get it? Do You really get how hard this life can be? Jesus, when no one else understands me, remind me that You do. Even though You are God, You lived on earth as a child and grew into a man. You experienced this life. You get it. Thanks, Jesus. Amen.

He had to be one of us, so he could serve God as our merciful and faithful high priest and sacrifice himself for the forgiveness of our sins.
HEBREWS 2:17 CEV

Day 207
CURB MY WORDS

Sometimes I blurt out things without thinking. I make a promise then I either forget it or I don't follow through. Other times, I retaliate and say things I shouldn't. In a rush of emotions, I make comments that are often unkind or disrespectful. That's not how I want to be, Lord. When You walked this earth, You watched Your words. You never reacted; You acted. Help me to choose my words wisely, to think before I speak, to thoughtfully consider before I make a promise. I want to become more like You. Thank You for loving me even when my tongue gets ahead of my thinking! Amen.

Do not be too hasty to speak your mind before God
or too quick to make promises you won't keep,
for God is in heaven and you are on earth.
Therefore, watch your tongue; let your words be few.
ECCLESIASTES 5:2 VOICE

BEAUTY FROM INSIDE

Creator God, show me what You see in me. Tell me how special I am to You. Help me to base my self-image on the way You see me. Your Word tells me that outward beauty doesn't last. Everyone ages. And true beauty comes from inside the heart. So help me to follow You with a servant's heart and to bless You no matter what! Help me to live my life for You and make me beautiful from the inside out. I know I'm worth a great deal to You. You gave Your life for me, after all! Amen.

Charm is deceptive, and beauty does not last;
but a woman who fears the Lord will be greatly praised.
PROVERBS 31:30 NLT

Day 209
NUMBER ONE

Father, thank You for not having favorites. I can run to You and know that You always have time for me and love me unconditionally because all Your children are number one to You. Help me to continue doing my best, knowing it's for You. . .and that You're the only one who really matters. I don't want to keep trying to do better and better, only to fail again. But in Your eyes, I'm not a failure! On days when I get discouraged, I ask that You comfort me in the way that only a best friend can. Thank You, Lord. Amen.

"Look at the birds of the air: they neither sow nor reap
nor gather into barns, and yet your heavenly Father
feeds them. Are you not of more value than they?"
MATTHEW 6:26 ESV

Day 210
AS PURE AS SNOW

Father, I know the Bible says You want us to be pure, not just in our hearts, but in our outward appearance—the way we dress ourselves. Help me not to fall into the trap of wanting to dress like other girls if it's not pleasing to You. And God, please work in my heart to keep it pure. My thoughts and attitudes need to be holy and as white as snow. I want You to look at me and smile because You're so pleased with how pure my heart is. Remind me every day, Lord, that staying in Your Word is the very best way to keep my heart innocent and clean. Amen.

How can a young person stay on the path of purity? By living according to your word.
PSALM 119:9 NIV

Day 211
AN ATTITUDE OF GRATITUDE

Heavenly Father, sometimes I find myself complaining about things or just being ungrateful in general. Whenever I'm behaving this way, help me to be thankful for everything I *do* have and for how You have taken care of me in the past. Thank You for my family, my friends, and for all the ways You have blessed me. Thank You for creating this beautiful world and giving me a place to live. Thank You for creating me just the way I am. Most of all, thank You for dying for my sins and giving me eternal life and the opportunity to share Your love with those around me. Amen.

Let your roots grow down into him, and let your lives be built on him. Then your faith will grow strong in the truth you were taught, and you will overflow with thankfulness.

COLOSSIANS 2:7 NLT

Day 212
SPEAK UP!

Lord, I love You with all my heart. But sometimes it's hard to talk about You in front of my friends. They don't all feel the same about You, and if I talk about You too much, they might think I'm weird. It's not that I'm ashamed of You, Lord. I just don't always know how to bring You into the conversation. Help me, Lord. Guide my words, my body language, my tone of voice. Help me know when to speak and when to stay quiet, showing Your love through my actions. Give me courage to talk about You and wisdom with the words I say. I want my words to point people to You. Amen.

"I tell you," he replied, "if they keep quiet, the stones will cry out."
LUKE 19:40 NIV

Day 213
HONOR IS REQUIRED

Today, Lord, I want to honor my parents by being obedient and respectful. I may not agree with their decisions, but help me not to be sassy or bratty—even behind their backs. Lord, You are the one who created families. You knew that kids couldn't make it on their own, and so You gave them parents to raise them. You are my heavenly Father, and I'm so glad to belong to Your family too. I ask You today to bless my mom and dad, even if they don't know You, and help me to honor them so we will all be closer to one another and to You. Amen.

"Honor your father and your mother, as the
Lord your God has commanded you."
DEUTERONOMY 5:16 NKJV

Day 214
SLOW TO SPEAK

Lord, words are powerful; they can wound so easily. So, when things don't go the way I want them to, help me to calm myself down by taking a few deep breaths and whispering Your name. Help me to come from a place of peace before I open my mouth. Give me the wisdom, Lord, to choose my words with care—or perhaps to just remain silent until I've thought things through a little more. Remind me that You would have me be quick to listen. Then—*and only then*—to speak. Amen.

Remember this, my dear friends! Everyone must be quick to listen, but slow to speak and slow to become angry. Human anger does not achieve God's righteous purpose.
JAMES 1:19–20 GNT

Day 215

HOW DID I END UP HERE?

Thank You for giving me the family that You knew I needed, Father. When I begin to question why I don't have a different type of family, teach me to trust in Your sovereignty. You don't make mistakes! I truly want to honor You in the way that I treat each member of my family. Even if they do not always treat me with respect, allow me to find it in my heart to show love, generosity, and genuine care. I love You, heavenly Father, and while no family is perfect, I thank You for choosing this one for me. It would be awfully lonely to live without a family. Amen.

God sets the lonely in families.
PSALM 68:6 NIV

Day 216
BE STILL

Lord, I don't want to miss out on anything. I don't want to quit the things that are important to me. At the same time, I need a break. I need a rest. It feels like I never have time to just relax.

You told us to be still, Lord. That sounds good, but to be honest, I don't know if I can. I want to take a break, but my mind just keeps going and going, even when my body gets still. Help me to be still and just listen to You, Lord. Thank You for holding me close and for teaching me what it means to be calm and rest in You. Amen.

"Be still, and know that I am God."
PSALM 46:10 NIV

Day 217
GOSSIP—NOT COOL!

Father, I don't want to gossip, so please help me to avoid others who spread rumors about everyone and everything! They're not my friends. Instead, I desire to become a good example. It seems that us females especially love to gossip. Although I'm not sure why, it's the way it is. But as a child of Yours, I know that You expect more from me. My desire is to obey You, not my foolish thoughts and ramblings. It's not cool to bad-mouth someone else behind her back. Give me the courage to silence the gossiper and my own temptations to gossip. Amen.

A gossip betrays a confidence,
but a trustworthy person keeps a secret.
PROVERBS 11:13 NIV

Day 218
HEAVEN'S REWARD

I've been so busy, Lord. Help me to slow down and keep my priorities straight. School, grades, friends, and college are all good things to strive toward, but I know this is all just a journey that will lead me to eternity with You. Help me to keep my heart set on that as I accomplish goals here on earth. Help me to do my best work, Lord. I want all this to be for Your glory, not mine. Thank You that You have set eternity right here in my heart (Ecclesiastes 3:11). Allow me to keep heaven in my mind during each task and milestone. Amen.

Work willingly at whatever you do, as though you were working for the Lord rather than for people. Remember that the Lord will give you an inheritance as your reward, and that the Master you are serving is Christ.
COLOSSIANS 3:23–24 NLT

Day 219
WAIT!

Father, some days it feels like everything is moving so slowly. I have tons of things to do, and it never seems like there's enough time. I guess I should be patient, Lord, but that's so much easier to say than do. Maybe I'm moving too fast. Please help me to learn to slow down, Jesus. Let me take a breath and learn how to wait. A lot of good things take time: flowers growing, good friendships forming, even a cake baking. None of that can be hurried. Help me to be patient like You want me to be. Amen.

See how the farmer waits for the precious fruit of the earth, being patient about it, until it receives the early and the late rains. You also, be patient.
JAMES 5:7–8 ESV

Day 220
GETTING MY WAY

Boy am I stubborn sometimes, Lord! I want to stomp my foot when I don't get my own way, to demand that people give me what I want. And if they don't give it to me, sometimes my attitude really stinks. Can You help me with this. . .please? Jesus didn't demand His own way. He prayed and asked His Father (You!) what to do. . .then He did it. No arguments. No foot stomping. He listened and then obeyed. I want to be like Jesus, Father! That means I must get rid of my pride. No more demanding. No more foot stomping. From now on, Lord, I will watch my attitude and humble myself. Amen.

Pride goes before destruction,
a haughty spirit before a fall.
PROVERBS 16:18 NIV

Day 221
ENVY

God, help me to be content with the things that I do have and to be thankful for having so much when so many people in the world have so little. Thank You for giving me parents who provide for me and take care of my needs. I know that true happiness and joy don't come from what I have—they come from walking with You and looking at everything in my life with gratitude. So the next time one of my friends gets new clothes or a new phone, remind me to be happy for her and not compare what she has with what I have. Amen.

I realized the reason people work hard and try to succeed: They are jealous of each other. This, too, is useless, like chasing the wind.

ECCLESIASTES 4:4 NCV

Day 222
SURPRISES AND WONDERS

Each and every day, Lord, renew my mind. Keep me from blindly following the latest fad or idol. Instead of worshipping the things and people of this world, I want to worship You alone. With my eyes on You, I know I will be following Your direction for my life. Open my ears to Your words and give me courage to walk the path You have laid out for me. If I take a course that seems different to others, I'm okay with that, because I know You will always be with me no matter what I do or where I go. Thank You for leading me *Your* way. Amen.

Do not conform to the pattern of this world, but be
transformed by the renewing of your mind. Then you
will be able to test and approve what God's will is.
ROMANS 12:2 NIV

Day 223
WHAT ABOUT ME?

Heavenly Father, Your Word reminds us that we should keep on doing good. You promise to reward us for all our effort (Galatians 6:9). Because of Your promise, Father, I'm asking that You help me to keep my focus on others instead of myself. I know You always see what I do to make a difference in the world, even when others don't see or don't care. And if You see, then that's enough for me! When others overlook or forget my kindness, it is so wonderful to know that You never will! Please help me to keep up the good work, God. And I'll be looking to see what good things You have in store for me. Amen.

Let us not become weary in doing good, for at the proper time we will reap a harvest if we do not give up.
GALATIANS 6:9 NIV

Day 224
LOVE ONE ANOTHER

Help me, Father, to remember how much You love me. While I was yet a sinner, You sent Jesus to earth. You allowed Your only Son to die a terrible death on the cross that I might have life. He went to the cross in my place! You love me *that* much! When others leave me out or hurt my feelings, let me react in love. When I am in a bad mood, help me to control my tongue. I want to be a person who is known for her love. I want to outdo everyone in showing love and respect, going beyond what is expected. Give me this type of heart, I pray, Lord.

Love one another with brotherly affection.
Outdo one another in showing honor.
ROMANS 12:10 ESV

Day 225
A TRUE FRIEND

Help me to be a good friend, Father. I want to be a good listener and someone who is trustworthy. Teach me to compromise with my friends. Make me the type of friend who respects others, not someone who is two-faced, acting one way in my friend's presence and then talking bad about her behind her back. God, You have blessed me with some good friends. Help me to be thankful for them and to treat them kindly even when we disagree. And where there is a need in my life for a friend, lead me to one who will be a true friend to me. I need wisdom as I choose godly friends. Amen.

Then Jonathan made a covenant with David
because he loved him as himself.
1 Samuel 18:3 NASB

Day 226
WHAT'S IMPORTANT

Even though I can't see You, God, I know You are there. I know You are good and You love me beyond what I can imagine. I want to know You better. Your Word tells me who You are, and the truth found there helps me understand more about You. I know there are a lot of opinions about who You are, and there are many people who can help me learn, but I need to go to the source—You. There is so much I don't know and can't understand about You, God! But thank You for giving us the Bible to read. Give me more understanding of who You are. Amen.

"Yes, a person is a fool to store up earthly wealth but not have a rich relationship with God."
LUKE 12:21 NLT

Day 227

WHAT ABOUT POPULARITY?

Popularity—what do You think of that, Lord? To me, popularity means other people like to be around me or think I'm pretty. Yet, when I read the Word of God, it never encourages this kind of popularity. Instead, You are pleased with a teachable, loving, compassionate, understanding, and Christ-centered heart and life. When I seek popularity, Father, I want to achieve the kind that Your followers had. I want others to look at me and see You—not what clothes I'm wearing or how pretty I am. Inner beauty remains forever—and that's the kind of popularity I desire, Lord. Amen.

I thank God for giving Titus. . . . He was most considerate of how we felt. . . . We're sending a companion along with him, someone very popular in the churches for his preaching of the Message. But there's far more to him than popularity. He's rock-solid trustworthy. The churches handpicked him to go with us.
2 CORINTHIANS 8:16–19 MSG

GOD IS LOVE

Loving You, God, shows the rest of the world that I am Yours and You are mine. I am so thankful that You sent Your Son to die in my place and take all the sin and shame for all my past, present, and future mistakes. You've paid for them all! I just can't wrap my brain around that. But I'm so very thankful. And by asking You to make Your home inside my heart, You gave me Your Spirit to lead me and guide me on my way to eternity with You. What a miracle! Thank You! Amen.

Whoever does not love does not know God, because God is love. This is how God showed his love among us: He sent his one and only Son into the world that we might live through him.
1 JOHN 4:8–9 NIV

Day 229
EVERYDAY BLESSINGS

Father, thank You for the many good things You give to me and do for me! I just love sleepovers with friends and laughing with them until my face hurts. I love all the shades of a beautiful sunset. I appreciate a new pair of shoes. . .especially if there was a really good sale! I love a warm drink on a cold day. I love birthday parties and spending time with those who are important to me. All of these good things—and more!—come from You, Lord Jesus. I have done nothing to deserve them, but You have given them to me anyway. You are so good! Thank You! Amen.

How great is your goodness that you have stored up for those who fear you, that you have given to those who trust you. You do this for all to see.
PSALM 31:19 NCV

Day 230
WHAT JOY!

Heavenly Father, I want my heart to be filled with joy. When people look at me, I want them to say, "Wow! She is always smiling! She seems so full of joy and life." I know that true joy comes from spending time with You, Father. Remind me of that when I start to feel down. Don't let me slip too far away from You. Keep my heart close to Yours so that Your joy will fill me up, bubbling inside of me until it spills over onto everything around me. What fun that will be, to live a joyous life! Amen.

Above all else, guard your heart,
for everything you do flows from it.
PROVERBS 4:23 NIV

Day 231
MY TEMPLE

Dear God, I want to take better care of myself—not just to look pretty but to be healthy and honor the body that You have created and given me. So please help me to have self-control when it comes to taking care of my body and making sure that I am treating it with the respect it deserves. I want to glorify You with every action I make. Continue to teach me how to do that. Amen.

You surely know that your body is a temple where the Holy Spirit lives. The Spirit is in you and is a gift from God. You are no longer your own. God paid a great price for you. So use your body to honor God.
1 CORINTHIANS 6:19–20 CEV

Day 232
BEING BEAUTIFUL

Dear God, I want to be beautiful. I don't think any girl *doesn't* want to be beautiful. You created us with the desire for beauty; You made us to bring beauty to Your world. But You also made us to be Yours first. Our beauty is to reflect Your glory. So, help me remember to pray about how I dress and behave. Help me remember to ask for Your guidance. God, I know that beauty in the soul is the thing that will last forever; develop in me a beautiful spirit and help me to honor You with my face and body all the days of my life. Amen.

You should clothe yourselves instead with the beauty that comes from within, the unfading beauty of a gentle and quiet spirit, which is so precious to God.
1 PETER 3:4 NLT

Day 233
FUTURE FRIENDS

Sometimes I fight with them and sometimes I stick up for them, but Lord, my siblings are here to stay. We're part of the same family, yet we're very different. They really bug me sometimes. My mom says that someday we'll be good friends, and I hope so—but it's hard to imagine that right now. Maybe one of the reasons You put me into a family is so I would learn to share and think about somebody besides myself. Even though I don't get along with them all the time, I do love my siblings, and I want us to have a good relationship someday. Amen.

A friend is always loyal, and a brother
is born to help in time of need.
PROVERBS 17:17 NLT

Day 234
LIKE AN EAGLE

Lord, every once in a while, when I'm trying to do something—get good grades, do well in sports, or serve You—I get frustrated, tired, and want to give up. Give me the strength to keep trying. If I stumble and fall, pick me up off the ground. Don't let me get down on myself but help me rise to the next challenge that comes my way. Give me the energy to soar like an eagle, going above the clouds, and rising to meet Your love and power. The more I practice flying, the stronger my wings will become and the better I will be able to serve You. Amen.

Even youths grow tired and weary, and. . .stumble and fall; but those who hope in the LORD will renew their strength. They will soar on wings like eagles; they will run and not grow weary, they will walk and not be faint.
ISAIAH 40:30–31 NIV

Day 235

DECISIONS BIG AND SMALL

Father God, some decisions are easy—like what to eat for breakfast, wear to school, or choose for dessert. Then there are the harder decisions—like what career I should pursue, what I should study for that next test, or what after-school activities to sign up for. Sometimes it takes me so long to figure out what I want to do or what I *should* do—that I miss out on awesome opportunities. Next time I have a decision to make, Lord, remind me to ask You for Your thoughts. Because You have *all* the answers! I know You will show me the right way to go—no matter if the decision is big or small. Amen.

Guide me by your truth and instruct me.
You keep me safe, and I always trust you.
PSALM 25:5 CEV

Day 236
NO FEAR

So much is going on in this world, God, and sometimes I feel afraid. The weight of all this worry presses down on me. I can't stop thinking about it. I know that King David, though he was a mighty warrior, was sometimes afraid too. In Psalm 56:3 (NLT) he says, "But when I am afraid, I will put my trust in you." Can it be that simple? To trust You to keep me and my family safe? I don't have control of the circumstances in my life, but I can choose how I will respond to them. David decided not to let fear control him. Don't let it control me either, God. Amen.

You can go to bed without fear; you will lie down and sleep soundly. You need not be afraid of sudden disaster or the destruction that comes upon the wicked, for the LORD is your security. He will keep your foot from being caught in a trap.
PROVERBS 3:24–26 NLT

Day 237
I WILL COMPLETE THIS!

Lord, sometimes I'm into my work, eager and ready to do well. I start a school project, enthusiastic and excited, only to feel differently when the project becomes difficult. Or I start to clean or decorate my room only to give up halfway. The scriptures tell me to finish what I start; to keep going when I want to give up; to complete any task to the best of my abilities. Help me, Father, when I'm tempted to quit, especially when I'm doing things I don't particularly like to do in the first place—like unloading the dishwasher! Amen.

The best thing you can do right now is to finish what you started. . .and not let those good intentions grow stale. Your heart's been in the right place all along. You've got what it takes to finish it up, so go to it.
2 CORINTHIANS 8:10–11 MSG

FOOD AND CLOTHES

God, it seems many of the girls around me obsess over diet and clothes. I get caught up in it too—comparing myself with other girls. And clothes! I'm always checking the mirror and wishing I had new things or trying on outfits and hoping my friends don't realize I wore the same thing just last week. When I begin to obsess, remind me of this: my life and my body were created by You to carry out Your plans for my life. Worrying about clothes and food is not pleasing to You. Help me to have a good balance. Help me not to worry about little stuff that doesn't really matter. Amen.

Jesus said, "That is why I tell you not to worry about everyday life—whether you have enough food to eat or enough clothes to wear. For life is more than food, and your body more than clothing."
LUKE 12:22–23 NLT

Day 239
THE ROUGH PLACES

Lord, I know You never promised life would be fair. As a matter of fact, it seems like the more difficult stuff we go through, the more we must depend on You to help us deal with it. And that makes us better people. I always want to pray for things to go smoothly in my life, Lord. But I wonder if it is the rough places that help smooth out my character. I'm *not* going to ask You to make my life hard, Lord. But I will pray that You use the difficult things in my life to make me more like You. Make me kinder, gentler, and more loving so I can make a positive difference in this world. Amen.

Count it all joy, my brothers, when you meet trials of various kinds, for you know that the testing of your faith produces steadfastness. And let steadfastness have its full effect, that you may be perfect and complete, lacking in nothing.
JAMES 1:2–4 ESV

Day 240
LOVELY PETALS

Lord, sometimes I think my relationship with You is like a flower opening up on a sunny day. That sweet little flower starts as a teeny-tiny seed that's planted deep in the ground, protected by the soil around it. After some time goes by, little green sprouts grow up out of the soil. Before long, a tightly closed bud appears on the vine. It drinks in the sun and water, preparing itself for what's about to come. Then, finally, the bud opens up for everyone to see—a gorgeous flower!

I'm like that flower, Father! When I gave You my heart, You planted a little seed of faith and now it's growing, growing, growing! Thank You, Lord. Amen.

And we know that in all things God works for the good of those who love him, who have been called according to his purpose.
ROMANS 8:28 NIV

Day 241
WHEN I NEED COURAGE

Lord, I sometimes get scared so easily. Sometimes I still imagine there is a monster under my bed, and I don't want to put my feet down in the dark! And then there are real fears, like when I go to a new school, and I don't know anyone. In situations like these, You always come to my rescue! You give me courage in every situation; I just need to call on You, and You are there. Thank You for Your promise to give me courage when I need it and for reminding me that You are always by my side. Amen.

But Jesus immediately said to them:
"Take courage! It is I. Don't be afraid."
MATTHEW 14:27 NIV

Day 242
NEVER DISAPPOINTED

Sometimes my life feels like one big disappointment after another, Lord. I hate feeling disappointed all the time. I want to feel happy and excited about life, but it's hard when things don't go my way. You said to put my hope in You. And Your love never changes. Your goodness never fails. Your kindness continues forever. I guess if I stop counting on things I can't control for my happiness and start counting on You alone, my attitude might change. I know that no matter how life disappoints me, You will always be there pouring beautiful things into my life. Thank You, Father! Amen.

"Then you will know that I am the Lord;
those who hope in me will not be disappointed."
ISAIAH 49:23 NIV

Day 243
ORDINARY DAYS

God, today I feel down, and I'm not sure why. There isn't really anything wrong, but I'm bored and feel stuck. I don't like ordinary days, but I know that ordinary days were common in the Bible too. It wasn't every day that the Red Sea parted, or lions' mouths were shut, or giants were slayed. Most days were simply ordinary. I think I'd like to have exciting things happen all the time, but maybe that wouldn't be good for me. I need to learn to follow You in everyday stuff so I'll be ready when the big stuff happens. Thank You for being there in all my very ordinary—and sometimes extraordinary—days. Amen.

Surely your goodness and unfailing love will pursue me all the days of my life.
PSALM 23:6 NLT

Day 244
QUIETLY HOPING

Sometimes I want answers *now*, Lord. I just don't want to wait. But when I am patient, really seek out Your Word and will, and look for Your help, hard times don't seem so hard. It's all about trusting You. Once I can get that idea in my head, I'm ready to do some more waiting. To be patient, quietly hoping in You, certain that You'll work everything out someday, somehow. You will find a way to bless me if my heart is in the right place, my mind calm, my spirit hopeful, and my faith sure. Thank You, Lord, for what You are about to do—today and tomorrow.

GOD proves to be good to the man who passionately waits, to the woman who diligently seeks. It's a good thing to quietly hope, quietly hope for help from GOD. It's a good thing when you're young to stick it out through the hard times.
LAMENTATIONS 3:25 MSG

Day 245
A TRUE DAUGHTER

I know that if I pray for the power to love others, Lord—friends *and* enemies—I am sure to receive it. So, help me today. Give me the strength to love *all* people. Give me the words to speak when I encounter those who have bullied me—and the words to pray when I think of them. I want to be like You, Jesus. I want a heart as big as Yours. Give me the peace that goes beyond all understanding. Make me royalty—a true daughter of You, my King and Father in heaven. Mold me into a princess of peace with love and prayers for all. Amen.

---

*"You have heard the law that says, 'Love your neighbor'
and hate your enemy. But I say, love your enemies!
Pray for those who persecute you! In that way, you will
be acting as true children of your Father in heaven."*
MATTHEW 5:43–45 NLT

Day 246

YOU KNOW ME

God, You know me better than I know myself! You know when I stand up and when I sit down—you know what I'm thinking before I even say it (Psalm 139). Being known *that* well might seem kind of risky. There is nothing hidden from You, God. Nothing surprises You. Yet You love me—no matter what I do. This only makes me want to love You back! Like the psalmist, I'm asking for Your guidance and direction, for You to show me the way to love You more. Give me eyes to see like You see me, God. Show me what I need to keep doing and what I need to change. Amen.

Search me, O God, and know my heart; test me and know my anxious thoughts. Point out anything in me that offends you, and lead me along the path of everlasting life.
PSALM 139:23–24 NLT

Day 247

MY HEAVENLY FATHER KNOWS BEST

Sometimes I think I know what's best. I want to make all my decisions by myself. Forgive me when I think that I know better than my parents—or You! When I try to figure out everything on my own, I usually get even more confused and frustrated. The truth is, I need my parents' advice and guidance, and I need Yours. I guess trusting You and my parents means allowing You to work in my life without my constant interference. I know that You and my parents are only trying to keep me on the right course. Remind me of that when I think I know what's best for me. Amen.

Trust God from the bottom of your heart; don't try to figure out everything on your own. Listen for God's voice in everything you do, everywhere you go; he's the one who will keep you on track. Don't assume that you know it all.
PROVERBS 3:5–6 MSG

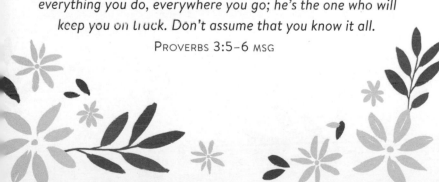

Day 248
PEACE AND THANKFULNESS

Father God, please give me a heart full of peace and thankfulness. What a difference I could make in my family and school if I always lived my life with a thankful heart! And if I let peace take control in my soul, not worrying about things that don't matter and trusting You no matter what happens?... My friends and family would take notice. They would see Your real power shining through me! I'm so glad You have my heart, Lord. We'll get through this life with peace and thankfulness ...*together*! Amen.

And let the peace that comes from Christ rule in your hearts. For as members of one body you are called to live in peace. And always be thankful.
Colossians 3:15 nlt

Day 249
HELP!

Lord, I get really stressed sometimes. I begin to worry, and then my heart starts to race, my palms get sweaty, and I feel like it's difficult to breathe. The stress comes when I begin taking the test that I studied hours for, but then find that I must not have studied the right material. The tension builds when I need to get up and talk in front of people. Father, I don't want to be ruled by stress. I need to learn to turn to You in those moments and ask You for help. You have promised to hear me, to help me, and to give me peace. Thank You! In Jesus' name, amen.

Commit everything you do to the LORD.
Trust him, and he will help you.
PSALM 37:5 NLT

Day 250
SASSY!

Lord, I can be the "Smart-Off Queen" sometimes! I don't mean to be so cranky, but sometimes it happens. When it does, I wind up in trouble and feeling ashamed. I know I look bad when I don't pay attention to how I speak to others—especially adults. Calm me down from the inside out. Put Your hand over my mouth so I don't say too much or speak in anger. I see better days ahead, Father! You are controlling my heart and my mouth. You're calming my heart when I get worked up. You're reminding me every time I get "sassy" that it breaks Your heart. You're never sassy with me, after all! Amen.

Set a guard, O Lord, over my mouth;
keep watch over the door of my lips!
Psalm 141:3 esv

Day 251

I'M NOT STRONG ENOUGH

Heavenly Father, sometimes I feel like I can't do something, like when I need to forgive a friend, and I just don't think I can do it alone. When I feel this way, I need to talk to You and ask You to give me the strength and the ability to forgive. You are my rock and my refuge. Thank You for always giving me strength when I think that what I'm trying to accomplish is beyond me; I don't know what I would do without Your presence in my life and Your hand guiding me through all the ups and downs. Thankfully, I never have to worry about that! Amen.

It is God who arms me with strength and keeps my way secure.
PSALM 18:32 NIV

Day 252
SING A SONG

Singing along with the radio may be fun, Lord, but it's not the same as having a song in my heart. Having a song in my heart means I'm thinking about You and praising You all the time. Having a song in my heart means I'm happy with who You are and who I am in You. It means that even when I'm thinking about other things, You're always there in the back of my mind. During my lifetime, I'll probably know the words to hundreds of songs. I'll probably forget the words to hundreds more. But one thing will remain, and that's Your love for me. That's something worth singing about! Amen.

Sing and make music from your heart to the Lord.
EPHESIANS 5:19 NIV

Day 253
CHOOSING FRIENDS

Thank You, Jesus, for my friends. They are there for me on the hard days and the fun days. I'm glad that I have friends to hang out with. I want to have good friends, and I want to be a good friend. Give me wisdom so I can choose wisely—help me observe the things they like, the attitudes they have, and what they post on Twitter and Facebook before I decide to hang out with them. I want to be smart in choosing friends because if I stay friends with them, I will become like them. Thank You for Your guidance. Amen.

Do not be misled: "Bad company corrupts good character."
1 Corinthians 15:33 niv

Day 254
TRUE SUCCESS

Success can mean so many different things to so many different people. To You, Lord, true success means going all out for You! It means reading or thinking about Your Word day and night, looking for Your direction, doing what You want me to do, and imitating Your Son, Jesus. If I do those things, I not only will be wise, making the right decisions, but will be seeing everything and everyone with Your eyes. In other words, I will see the good in all things. So Lord, I pray that You will help me to prosper in all I do, think, and say. Make me Your success story. Amen.

This Book of the Law shall not depart out of your mouth, but you shall meditate on it day and night, that you may observe and do according to all that is written in it. For then you shall make your way prosperous, and then you shall deal wisely and have good success.
JOSHUA 1:8 AMPC

Day 255
GOD'S PLANS

Heavenly Father, just as a jigsaw puzzle is put together one piece at a time, You will show me the next step to take at just the right time. I can imagine You gazing upon the whole puzzle, already intact. You can see the beautiful picture that one day will be revealed to me. For now, I will just live this day for You. I will walk and talk with You. I will read Your Word and follow Your commands. Thank You for the knowledge that You have plans full of hope and goodness for me! Amen.

"For I know the plans I have for you," says the LORD. "They are plans for good and not for disaster, to give you a future and a hope."
JEREMIAH 29:11 NLT

Day 256
BEAUTY

The world is so different from You, God! TV and magazines say that to be beautiful you have to be a certain size or wear the newest fashion. Even at school there seems to be a club of "beautiful people," and I don't fit in it. Is it possible they are wrong? You created me, so I must be beautiful! Lord, I want to believe I'm beautiful, but *feeling* beautiful is a different story. The more I become like You, the more beautiful I will be. Make me beautiful on the inside, Lord. Amen.

Christ's love makes the church whole. His words evoke her beauty. Everything he does and says is designed to bring the best out of her, dressing her in dazzling white silk, radiant with holiness.
Ephesians 5:26–27 msg

Day 257
I CAN TRUST GOD

Some days I am unsure of who I can *really* trust, Lord. What I know for sure, though, is that I *can* trust You. I can come to You with anything, and You will listen, guide, and help me. Thank You, God, that I can share anything with You. Your Word is true, and I can trust Your promises. When I feel that no one is trustworthy, remind me that You are. You will never fail me, and You will never turn Your back on me. Forgive me when I don't trust You as I should. I want to trust and become trustworthy, just as You are. Amen.

Your kingdom is an everlasting kingdom, and your dominion endures through all generations. The LORD is trustworthy in all he promises and faithful in all he does.
PSALM 145:13 NIV

THE UNSEEN

Even though I've never seen You and have never heard Your voice out loud, I trust in the words of the Bible, and I have faith that You are with me. All I need to do some days is get outside and look at the beauty of Your creation. The sky and the trees and all the living things You created. Life came from You alone, God. I know that with all my heart. You've filled me with joy because You've given me eternal life. My purpose is to live out my life loving You and pointing others to You. Amen.

Though you have not seen him, you love him; and even though you do not see him now, you believe in him and are filled with an inexpressible and glorious joy, for you are receiving the end result of your faith, the salvation of your souls.

1 PETER 1:8–9 NIV

Day 259
TEMPTATION

God, temptation is all around me. I pray that You will give me power to say no to the things that do not honor or please You, Father. I read of Bible heroes who trusted You and who did not give in to temptation. Their lives were truly blessed. Those who gave in to temptation were given another chance, but they often had to live with tough consequences for their sins. Help me to choose right over wrong. Be at my side and hold my hand. I think I can withstand temptation if I know that You are always with me, God. Amen.

You are tempted in the same way that everyone else is tempted. But God can be trusted not to let you be tempted too much, and he will show you how to escape from your temptations.

1 CORINTHIANS 10:13 CEV

Day 260
DROP IT!

You don't like me to hang on to hurt, Lord. . .for my sake and the sake of the person who hurt me. You want me to let it go, like the dog dropping the bone when his master commands him to.

Help me let go of the offenses. When my feelings are hurt, whisper, *"Drop it! Let it go!"* in my ear. And if I try to hang on to it, remind me that You had every reason to be offended when You sent Jesus to the world and the world rejected Him. You didn't get offended, though. You did just the opposite! You kept loving, kept forgiving, kept giving. May I learn from Your example, Father. Amen.

Good sense makes one slow to anger,
and it is his glory to overlook an offense.
PROVERBS 19:11 ESV

Day 261
LOVING YOU

Heavenly Father, I want to love and honor You in everything I do. I want to follow all Your commandments and walk in the ways that You have instructed, but I am so easily distracted by things on earth. I need to remind myself that You are the most important relationship in my life—nothing else compares. I need to remember to talk to You, listen for Your wisdom in my life, and just spend time being quiet in Your presence. Thank You for never growing impatient with me or giving up on me. I know that Your love is perfect and will never cease. Thank You for Your assurance and constant love. Amen.

We show our love for God by obeying his commandments, and they are not hard to follow. Every child of God can defeat the world, and our faith is what gives us this victory.
1 JOHN 5:3–4 CEV

Day 262
COOL STUFF

My parents can't buy me everything I want, Lord. They try to give me the best they can, but even I know the earthly gifts they give me won't last forever. The gifts You give, though, are perfect. They never wear out. Things like Your love, Your peace, Your joy—those are things money can't buy. They only come from You. I know the cool stuff I get comes from You. You give me everything I need—and many things I want. Thank You for giving me beautiful gifts. Help me to be grateful to my parents and to You. Help me remember that every good thing comes from You. Amen.

Every good and perfect gift is from above, coming down from the Father of the heavenly lights.

JAMES 1:17 NIV

Day 263
WHAT AN AWESOME IDEA!

Heavenly Father, I'm so glad You thought of the idea of church. There are different types of churches—some are large, others are small; some like hand-clapping and praise music, others prefer hymns. But the most important thing is that they proclaim Jesus is Lord and follow the teachings of the Bible. Thank You for the church—it's a place of learning and caring. I want to fill my place and be faithful to come and worship and praise. Bless my pastor today and help me make my church a better place. Amen.

Now you are the body of Christ,
and each one of you is a part of it.
1 CORINTHIANS 12:27 NIV

Day 264
PEACE VS. ENVY

Father, I never considered *peace* the opposite of *envy*. But the author of Proverbs makes it clear! Help me to be content with what I have and where I am in life. Jealousy is like a virus that spreads quickly throughout my entire being when I allow it. Envy is not from You, God. I know it is from the devil, who wants to capture my heart and mind with his deceptions. I pray that today You will plant a deep peace in my heart that says "I'm okay. I look the way God created me to look. I have a good family. And I don't need fancy, expensive things to make me happy." Peace versus envy? I choose peace. Amen.

A heart at peace gives life to the body, but envy rots the bones.
PROVERBS 14:30 NIV

Day 265
PRODUCING FRUIT

Reveal to me the gifts and abilities You have given me, Father. Help me to know how and where I can serve You best. As I go through my daily life, point out to me opportunities where I can work for Your kingdom. I want to be Your hands and feet. I want to love others in such a way that they recognize You and come to salvation. Help me always remain in close fellowship with You. I know that if I try to do the work on my own, it will be useless, but anything done in Your name will last. Amen.

"Yes, I am the vine; you are the branches.
Those who remain in me, and I in them, will produce
much fruit. For apart from me you can do nothing."
JOHN 15:5 NLT

WISDOM VS. FOOLISHNESS

Wisdom is doing the things I *know* I should do, but foolishness is found in going my own way, not God's. Job tells us that "God alone understands the way to wisdom; he knows where it can be found" (Job 28:23 NLT). I may have knowledge and know a lot, but I can't be wise on my own. Proverbs tells us that wisdom is sweet and brings hope and a bright future (see Job 24:14 NLT).

I need to learn wisdom, but I also need to learn to value having wisdom, God. Give me wisdom, God. Help me avoid being foolish. Amen.

Fear of the LORD is the foundation of true knowledge,
but fools despise wisdom and discipline.
PROVERBS 1:7 NLT

Day 267
CUTTING WORDS

I want to hold my tongue, yet sometimes I don't, Lord. I say things that aren't nice or that are even hurtful to others when someone treats me badly or upsets me. Yet my anger only makes matters worse than they already are. Please help me curb my anger at those times, Lord. Give me the self-control I need when I want to lash out. Substitute my otherwise cutting, harsh words and responses with words that will calm me and those around me. I am grateful that You are always kind and loving, even when I'm not. Help me to hold my tongue and answer with kindness as You would do. Amen.

A gentle answer deflects anger,
but harsh words make tempers flare.
PROVERBS 15:1 NLT

Day 268
DOING MY OWN THING

It's so hard not to want my own way, Father! I just want to ignore what my parents are telling me sometimes and do my own thing. When they give me instructions, I want to say no and do the opposite. I've been guilty of being immature sometimes. I know I can be a little rebellious, God. Please forgive me for that. I want to be a person who does what she's told without making a scene. I'm asking You to touch my heart today and get rid of any stubbornness inside of me. The Bible says that I should listen to the adults in my life. Help me to do that with a clean heart, Father. Amen.

Listen, my son, to your father's instruction and do not forsake your mother's teaching. They are a garland to grace your head and a chain to adorn your neck.
PROVERBS 1:8–9 NIV

Day 269
KEEPING MY WORD

Heavenly Father, I want people to know me as a person who is trustworthy—if I give my word, I'll keep my word. But if I begin making promises and going back on them, I will give others reason to doubt me. Lord Jesus, I ask for the wisdom to know when to give my word regarding something and when not to. Help me to weigh out the positives and negatives first, before committing to something. And then help me to follow through with my promise, even if it's inconvenient or difficult for me. In Your name, amen.

Many people claim to be loyal, but it is hard to find a trustworthy person.
PROVERBS 20:6 NCV

Day 270
THREE THINGS

I will keep the hope that You, Jesus, will give me the power to live this life in Your light. Hope that I will someday be reunited with loved ones who have gone to heaven before me. Hope that I will one day see Your shining face. And, even greater than faith and hope, I will live a life of love, reaching out to one and all with the love of Christ who gives me the strength to do what seems impossible. With my confident faith, trusting hope, and boundless love, I will live an amazing life, far above the troubles of this world. With these three things, I become one with You. Amen.

But now faith, hope, and love remain; these three virtues must characterize our lives. The greatest of these is love.
1 CORINTHIANS 13:13 VOICE

Day 271
LOVING OTHERS

Dear God, I don't always find it that easy to love others. You know my thoughts. You know how frustrated I get when I find others annoying or just want to be alone. I need to remember that everyone was created by You and is deserving of respect and love. Soften my heart toward those who are not easy to love and show me how to serve them with a willing heart. Let love show through my thoughts, words, and actions. Lord, You are the perfect example of love. Let me look to You whenever I am feeling empty and feel like it's impossible to love someone. Amen.

Dear friends, let us continue to love one another, for love comes from God. Anyone who loves is a child of God and knows God.
1 JOHN 4:7 NLT

Day 272
FAITH WITHOUT WORKS

I love You, God. Of course, I love You. If anyone asks me, I'll tell them right away. "I love God, and I have faith in Him." But I'm learning that words aren't enough. I can say I love You, but if my actions don't support my words, what's the point? Words alone don't mean a thing. Even my thoughts don't mean a whole lot if the way I live my life doesn't match my faith. Lord, help me to make my faith real. Help me to show, through every action, that I love You, I trust You, I honor You, and my hope is in You. Amen.

Faith by itself, if it does not have works, is dead.
JAMES 2:17 ESV

Day 273
A TRUE LADY

Dear God, I'm beginning to think that boys are sort of wonderful. When I was little, I thought they were gross and pests. But my attitude sure has changed a lot lately. I need Your wisdom so I will know how to dress and how to act around the young men in my life. Your Word calls that *discretion*. I need to know the difference between enjoying being around boys and encouraging wrong feelings. I want to be a young woman who makes You proud, Lord. Since I belong to You, I want You to be pleased with how I act. Amen.

A beautiful woman who lacks discretion
is like a gold ring in a pig's snout.
PROVERBS 11:?? NLT

Day 274
A THANKFUL HEART

God, today I am thankful for all that You have given me. Thank You for the people You have put in my life who truly care about me. Thank You for the education I am getting, which will help me to have a job where I can make a difference in the world. Thank You for my friends and family and my home. Thank You for the clothes I wear and the food I eat. I know that all these things come directly from Your hands. Help me to be content with all that You have blessed me with. Help me always to have a thankful heart. Amen.

Be thankful in all circumstances, for this is God's will for you who belong to Christ Jesus.
1 THESSALONIANS 5:18 NLT

Day 275
KIND, TENDERHEARTED, AND FORGIVING

This is my prayer today, heavenly Father: that in every difficult situation I face, I would seek out ways to be kind, to have tenderness in my heart toward others, and that I'd always be willing to forgive. You have forgiven me for a lot of things—help me to remember that when the time comes for me to forgive a friend for something in the future. I want to be a kind and tender girl—one who is known for being loving and Christlike. Thanks for giving me Your power and wisdom to guide me in all things. Amen.

Get rid of all bitterness, rage, anger, harsh words, and slander, as well as all types of evil behavior. Instead, be kind to each other, tenderhearted, forgiving one another, just as God through Christ has forgiven you.
EPHESIANS 4:31–32 NLT

Day 276
A HUGE PROMISE

I'm so thankful for Your Word, Lord! It gives me the answers I need for this life. Help me not to worry, but to pray when I feel nervous or anxious about anything. Help me to share my feelings with You as I feel them instead of holding them inside and getting even more stressed. I want to be thankful instead of stressful! When I give thanks to You instead of worrying, a very powerful thing happens that You've promised right here in Your Word: You'll give me peace! A peace that doesn't really make sense to anyone else but me. And You'll guard my heart and my mind as I live in You, Jesus. What a huge promise! Amen.

Do not worry. Learn to pray about everything. Give thanks to God as you ask Him for what you need. The peace of God is much greater than the human mind can understand. This peace will keep your hearts and minds through Christ Jesus.
PHILIPPIANS 4:6–7 NLV

Day 277
RADIANT

Lord, I heard someone describe a gorgeous actress as *radiant*. She was beautiful in her sparkly dress, and she looked really happy. She looked like the kind of person I could be friends with—the kind of person who would be nice to a stranger. I think that's what radiant means. . .it's a kind of pretty that comes from being happy and full of love. Lord, I want to look nice on the outside, but I don't want it to stop there. I want to shine with happiness and kindness and gentleness. I want to have the kind of beauty that draws people to me—the kind of beauty that comes from being like You. Help me to be radiant today, Lord. Amen.

Those who look to him are radiant.
PSALM 34:5 NIV

Day 278

SAVING FOR ETERNITY .

Please help me to be a good steward, Father. I know that means taking good care of the finances and things You've blessed me with here on earth. I know You don't want me to put all my hope in earthly treasures and lots of money. If I treasure any "thing" too much here on earth, it will take a hold of my heart in ways that aren't pleasing to You. Help me to store up treasures in heaven! The kind of treasures I'll receive in eternity for loving and serving You with all my heart—for doing things for others without recognition and without expecting anything in return. Amen.

"Do not store up for yourselves treasures on earth, where moths and vermin destroy, and where thieves break in and steal. But store up for yourselves treasures in heaven, where moths and vermin do not destroy, and where thieves do not break in and steal. For where your treasure is, there your heart will be also."
MATTHEW 6:19–21 NIV

Day 279

MAKING WISE DECISIONS

Lord Jesus, I need Your help in making wise choices. Although I have internal debates when it comes to making good choices, I really know the right answers, Father. Your Spirit tells me to avoid things I know are wrong, whether there is anyone around or not. It's so much easier to just give in, especially if I think I'll be made fun of if I don't. But obedience is much more important than trying to fit in. I want to make You happy, Jesus, no matter what that means to my reputation. Amen.

---

*Our only goal is to please God. . .because we must
all stand before Christ to be judged. Each of us
will receive what we should get—good or bad—
for the things we did in the earthly body.*
2 Corinthians 5:9–10 ncv

Day 280
OKAY IN MY OWN SKIN

God, can I admit something? Sometimes I'm not okay in my own skin. I'm really grateful You created me, and I know You want me to relax and be myself, but sometimes I just wish I could look like someone else or have the talents of someone else. It's not always easy to be me! Father, remind me that You created me in Your image. When You look at me, You don't compare me to others. I know Your Word says that You're crazy about me, just the way I am right now. Before I was ever born, You knew exactly what I would be like, and the Bible says that all of Your works are wonderful. Amen.

For you created my inmost being; you knit me together in my mother's womb. I praise you because I am fearfully and wonderfully made; your works are wonderful, I know that full well.
PSALM 139:13–14 NIV

Day 281
IF I HAD MY WAY

If I had my way, Lord, every day would be filled with smiles and laughter and happiness. Every day would be like a fairy tale, with birds singing and little animals dancing, and the bad would lose and the good would win. What's wrong with that, Lord? Then again, if there were no bad things, no disappointments in life, I guess I wouldn't really appreciate the good things. If all I ever knew were happiness and singing birds and rainbows, I'd have nothing to compare them with. Help me today to be grateful for even the hard things in life. They give me wisdom and bring me to a deeper appreciation of Your goodness. Amen.

Consider it pure joy, my brothers and sisters,
whenever you face trials of many kinds.
JAMES 1:2 NIV

WISDOM VS. KNOWLEDGE

Lord, it's good to have all the knowledge I can have. Knowledge will help me be successful in whatever I do in life. But if there's one thing that's more important than knowledge, it's wisdom. Knowledge is all about facts and figures and knowing how to do things. Wisdom is about making good life choices. Knowledge may teach me how to build a house, but wisdom will teach me to have a happy home. Knowledge may teach me the right medicines to use to clean a scratch on my knee, but wisdom shows me how to heal a heart. Father, give me Your wisdom so I can make good choices for my life. Amen.

If any of you lacks wisdom, you should ask God, who gives generously to all without finding fault, and it will be given to you.
JAMES 1:5 NIV

Day 283
MY BEST FRIEND

Lord, I have days when I feel like my friends don't understand or they can't relate to how I feel. Other "friends" are fake because they talk behind my back and change loyalties constantly. Although I realize that some friends will come and go in my life, help me to appreciate my true friends. Not only that, help me to become a dependable friend who others can trust. You, Father, are my very best friend. You are always with me to listen and help. You understand me even when I don't understand myself! You accept me as I am but love me too much to leave me that way. Jesus, thank You for being a true friend. Amen.

Some friends are fun to be with, but a true
friend can be better than a brother.
PROVERBS 18:24 ERV

A SECRET PLACE

Lord, when I am confident in You, totally trusting You for everything, all Your promises come true. Your angels lift me up, protecting and saving me from dangers I don't even see. I find comfort under Your enormous and all-powerful wings. Nothing can frighten me—neither tests, nor strangers, nor harmful words. When I am facing any kind of challenge, I merely call on You, and You come immediately to my rescue. You are my constant shield. As long as I am living in You, Your courage, Your peace, and Your power are mine. Thank You for being such an awesome God. Amen.

He who dwells in the secret place of the Most High shall remain stable and fixed under the shadow of the Almighty [Whose power no foe can withstand]. I will say of the Lord, He is my Refuge and my Fortress, my God; on Him I lean and rely, and in Him I [confidently] trust!
PSALM 91:1–2 AMPC

ALWAYS

God, I know that Your will is what is best for me. Help me to trust You as doors close in my life, that You will open the ones I need to journey through at just the right time. You are my loving heavenly Father who will never let me go. Thank You, God, for loving me with an everlasting love and blessing me with Your sweet kindness. It is only through Christ that I can come into Your presence. I am so thankful that we will be together always. Amen.

The LORD appeared to us in the past, saying:
"I have loved you with an everlasting love;
I have drawn you with unfailing kindness."
JEREMIAH 31:3 NIV

Day 286
DREAM BIG!

Maybe it is a little soon to know *exactly* what my whole future will look like, God, but I know that I want to choose Your plans over mine. I dream of doing great things one day—of being successful and living a life that counts for something. I need Your help to do that. Your Word tells me, "God has given each of you a gift from his great variety of spiritual gifts. Use them well to serve one another" (1 Peter 4:10 NLT). That means that I have gifts and strengths and talents too! Help me to figure out what those are and how to use them in ways that will honor You most. Amen.

God began doing a good work in you, and I am sure he will continue it until it is finished when Jesus Christ comes again.

PHILIPPIANS 1:6 NCV

CONSTRUCTIVE CRITICISM

Father, when my mom or dad tells me something about myself that I know is true and I need to change, give me the humility and ability to change my reaction to their comments. Help me to receive the truth and take it to You in prayer instead of allowing my hurt feelings to cause resentment. I know my parents love me and want what's best for me, just like You do, Lord. When they give me constructive criticism, it is only to help me become a better person, a better Christian. Help me to know that and act accordingly. Thank You, Lord, for loving and accepting me just as I am, but caring too much to leave me that way. Amen.

Remember what you are taught,
and listen carefully to words of knowledge.
PROVERBS 23:12 NCV

GOD IS AWAKE

I have a lot on my heart today, Lord Jesus. There are things in my life—and in this world—that hurt my heart. I'm coming to You because You tell me to come to You with my burdens and You will give me rest (Matthew 11:28). I am weary and burdened. This stuff feels heavy on my shoulders. Will You give me peace and rest tonight? Thank You that I can go to sleep knowing that You're watching over everything and that You're still awake, taking care of it all. Amen.

My help comes from the LORD, who made heaven and earth!
He will not let you stumble; the one who watches over you
will not slumber. Indeed, he who watches over Israel never
slumbers or sleeps. The LORD himself watches over you!
PSALM 121:2–5 NLT

Day 289
A PRINCESS, FOR REAL?

Heavenly Father, You not only call me Your princess; You call me an "heir of God's glory" (Romans 8:17 NLT). I'm an heir who gets to share in Your glory! I can only imagine how awesome Your glory is, but that You have chosen me, as Your follower, to share in that is beyond comprehension. Thank You for saving me from eternal death and for preparing a special place for me in Your heaven. I want to live my life for You out of a heart full of love. And one day, I will finally get to see the face of my eternal King. Thank You, Jesus! Amen.

But to all who believed him and accepted him,
he gave the right to become children of God.
JOHN 1:12 NLT

Day 290

TEARING UP THE PICTURE

Do You ever have a hard time forgiving people, God? I do. Your Word says that I should be quick to forgive because You were quick to forgive me. I guess that forgiving someone is kind of like tearing up the picture of what they did and throwing it in the trash. When I do that—when I let go of it—You are free to heal my heart. Yesterday is in the past. Today is what matters. Lord, You've already forgiven me for the sins I committed yesterday. Show me how to forgive others who have hurt me the same way You've already forgiven me. Amen.

"Come now, let's settle this," says the LORD. "Though your sins are like scarlet, I will make them as white as snow. Though they are red like crimson, I will make them as white as wool."
ISAIAH 1:18 NLT

Day 291
DAILY FAITH

Lord, when people in Sunday school talk about faith, it sounds so easy; I just must trust You to take care of everything, and You will. But I'm finding it is difficult to have constant faith in You. My first instinct is to have faith in my friends or in myself, or I constantly worry and don't trust You to provide for my needs. You have been so faithful to me in the past. Help me to remember that when I'm struggling with something new, and I don't turn to You or have faith that You can handle a situation. Thank You for always being faithful to me; I want to be faithful to You too. Amen.

It is written in the Scriptures, "I believed, so I spoke."
Our faith is like this, too. We believe, and so we speak.
God raised the Lord Jesus from the dead, and we know
that God will also raise us with Jesus. God will bring us
together with you, and we will stand before him.
2 CORINTHIANS 4:13–14 NCV

Day 292
MY WORDS

Lord, sometimes I can be sweet to a person's face, but say unkind things about them behind their backs. Sometimes I can pray and tell You how much I love You, God, and five minutes later I'll be saying or thinking something mean about one of Your children. I know that's wrong. Help me to love others with my words, whether it's to their faces or behind their backs. I want to be the kind of person others can count on, the kind of person others feel safe around. Give me wisdom, and help me control my tongue in a way that honors You. Amen.

Out of the same mouth come praise and cursing.
My brothers and sisters, this should not be.
JAMES 3:10 NIV

Day 293
PATIENCE

Lord, patience is a virtue—something to value and pursue. Your Word tells me that patience is a fruit of Your Spirit (Galatians 5:22). I guess that means I can't do it very well on my own—I need Your help! Patience is waiting for the right time for everything and trusting You for the result, not myself. Help me develop patience, God, to live fully in the "right now" of my life. To enjoy what I have and to be content to wait for what is ahead. I know You have the future under control and that You want what is best for me. Help me to appreciate all that You have for me now. Amen.

But let patience have its perfect work, that you may be perfect and complete, lacking nothing.
JAMES 1:4 NKJV

Day 294
GOD IN MY CORNER

I love the amazing stories in Your Word, Father God, especially when You show how powerful You are. There's one story about huge armies coming to fight King Jehoshaphat. Instead of totally panicking, Jehoshaphat ran straight to You and asked for help. And boy, did You give it! After lots of prayer and praise from Jehoshaphat and his people, You made the enemy armies attack each other. Not one hair on the heads of the Israelites was harmed. Not only that, but they ended up with all their enemies' treasures! When I come up against trouble, it's so comforting to know I have such a powerful God in my corner. Thank You, Father! Amen.

"You will not even need to fight. Take your positions; then stand still and watch the LORD's victory. He is with you. . . . Do not be afraid or discouraged. Go out against them tomorrow, for the LORD is with you!"
2 CHRONICLES 20:17 NLT

Day 295

THE NEW ME

Heavenly Father, I want to please You with my life. When I am around other Christians, I get so excited about Your Word. I love to sing praise and worship songs. But I find that when I am with non-Christians, it is harder to stand strong in my beliefs. I know that as a human being, it is impossible for me to be perfect. I am a sinner who has been saved by grace through faith in Your Son, Jesus. In Your power, I can make right choices and resist the urge to sin against You. Strengthen me, I pray. Help me to stand out in the crowd as a follower of Christ. Amen.

Those who are God's children do not continue sinning, because the new life from God remains in them. They are not able to go on sinning, because they have become children of God.
1 JOHN 3:9 NCV

Day 296
PRAISE

God, the psalms are filled with reasons to praise You. I know that You alone deserve all praise and honor. What surprises me is what praising *You* can do for *me*! Praising You brings hope and joy into my life. It brings confidence and trust. Praising You is just telling it like it is. You are wonderful and mighty. You are beyond my human understanding. When I praise You, my attitude about everything else changes. When I sing worship songs or tell others or remind myself of who You are and what You have done for me, my heart feels glad and it shifts my perspective. Thank You, Lord! Amen.

Let all that I am praise the LORD; may I never forget the good things he does for me.
PSALM 103:2 NLT

Day 297
SHOP WITH ME, LORD

Sometimes it's hard to avoid trendy clothing or brand names, Lord. So, when I shop, would You help me make the right choices to look attractive without giving in to the latest fashions that might be inappropriate for me to wear? I don't want a designer label to lure me into buying something that might be impressive but impractical. I ask You to guide me more toward serving You and less toward caring too much about how I appear on the exterior. I pray for a pure heart and proper attire that mirrors who a believer is inside and out. Amen.

Women, the same goes for you: dress properly, modestly, and appropriately. Don't get carried away in grooming your hair or seek beauty in glittering gold, pearls, or expensive clothes.
1 TIMOTHY 2:9 VOICE

Day 298
GOD IS SOVEREIGN

Lord, open my eyes to see You working in my life and in the lives of those around me. Open my ears to hear what You want to say to me through Your Word. Open my heart to fully experience the relationship that You long to have with me. Remind me that nothing can get in the way of Your love for me. You are sovereign, which means You have ultimate power and authority over everyone and everything. Don't allow me to be fooled into thinking anyone else has control over me or this world. You are God, and I'm not. And neither is anyone else. Thank You for caring so much for me. Amen.

For I am convinced that neither death nor life,
neither angels nor demons, neither the present nor the
future, nor any powers, neither height nor depth,
nor anything else in all creation, will be able to separate
us from the love of God that is in Christ Jesus our Lord.
ROMANS 8:38–39 NIV

Day 299
SOCIALLY ACCEPTABLE

Father, please guard my thoughts, my eyes, and my hands as I am on my phone. I love to have conversations with my friends, but sometimes it can get close to gossiping as we chat. Please keep me pure as I view and post photos. I know what's right and what's wrong, but sometimes, in the name of a joke, the line can be crossed. Help me to remember that I need to choose my words carefully and to only hit SEND or POST if I know what I've typed will please You. Once the words are "out there," I can never get them back. Please give me wisdom. Amen.

Let the words of my mouth and the meditation of my heart be acceptable in your sight, O LORD, my rock and my redeemer.
PSALM 19:14 ESV

Day 300
GOOD FRUIT

Heavenly Father, You tell me about spiritual fruit in Your Word, and it makes a lot of sense to me. A heart that is pleasing to You produces healthy, yummy fruit. A heart that is not following You produces rotten, bitter fruit. Please fill me with the kind of spiritual fruit that tastes good to others and is good for me. The Bible says there is no law against being loving or joyful or full of peace, patience, kindness, goodness, faithfulness, gentleness, and self-control. I'm not going to get into trouble with anybody for showing that kind of fruit. It's healthy for my body and my soul and will lead me closer in my relationship with You, God. Amen.

But the Holy Spirit produces this kind of fruit in our lives: love, joy, peace, patience, kindness, goodness, faithfulness, gentleness, and self-control. There is no law against these things!
GALATIANS 5:22–23 NLT

Day 301
BEING BEAUTIFUL

Heavenly Father, help me to remember that it is more important to be kind and loving, walking with You daily, than it is to be pretty. You designed me, and You find me beautiful even if I don't have perfect hair or blemish-free skin. You don't judge me based on how I look, so I don't want to judge anyone else based on their physical appearance, even if it's an easy thing to do. Please help me to love the body and the face that You have given me rather than focusing on everything that I want to change. May all my thoughts, words, and actions be glorifying to You. Amen.

Charm can be deceiving, and beauty fades away, but a woman who honors the LORD deserves to be praised.
PROVERBS 31:30 CEV

Day 302
PRAY FIRST

Sometimes I forget to pray, Lord. I know I'm praying right now, but many times when I'm faced with something challenging, I try to figure things out on my own. It's not wrong for me to try to figure things out, Lord. But I should pray first. It's not wrong to seek advice from friends, if I'm seeking Your advice first. Prayer should be my first option, not my last resort. There will always be troubles in my life, Lord. Every day I'll be faced with circumstances I don't know how to handle, problems I don't know how to fix. When these situations come up, help me remember to talk to You first before trying anything else. Amen.

Is anyone among you in trouble? Let them pray.
JAMES 5:13 NIV

Day 303
FAR DEEPER LOVE

Sometimes, Lord, people are just so hard to figure out. I think my friends are mad at me—but I have no idea why. Was it something I said or did? Or was it something I *didn't* say or do? All I know is that I feel like an outcast. With that in mind, I know nothing anyone says or does can really hurt me. So, Lord, lift my burdened heart. Clear the confusion from my mind. Give me bright hope for tomorrow. Fill me with the light of Your love and allow it to shine through me so that I can learn to love others—even when they seem not to love me.

No one has ever seen God. But if we love each other,
God lives in us, and his love is brought to full expression in us.
1 JOHN 4:12 NLT

Day 304
A GLIMPSE OF GOD

I know that I am a work in progress, Lord. Every day I am changing more and more into the woman I will be someday. In the meantime, though, I know I need to treat my body right. Help me to remember that my body really isn't my own—it's Yours. Give me the wisdom to treat it right. Help me to feed my mind, body, and spirit in such a way that when people see me, they will catch a glimpse of You. Amen.

Didn't you realize that your body is a sacred place, the place of the Holy Spirit? Don't you see that you can't live however you please, squandering what God paid such a high price for? The physical part of you is not some piece of property belonging to the spiritual part of you. God owns the whole works. So let people see God in and through your body.
1 CORINTHIANS 6:19–20 MSG

Day 305
FITTING IN

God, lately it seems as if I just don't "fit in." I am just always sort of in between. I'm not the least popular, but certainly not the most popular. I do have some friends. I just never feel like I am part of the "right" crowd. I guess as a Christian, I am not really meant to fit in here on earth. I am supposed to be different. Help me, God, to find Christian friends who I can relate to and mature with. If they are already in my life, help me to recognize their great value. I need to just rest in Your arms right now, Lord. I belong to You. You are where I fit in. Amen.

But our citizenship is in heaven. And we eagerly
await a Savior from there, the Lord Jesus Christ.
PHILIPPIANS 3:20 NIV

Day 306
SO MANY DUMB MOMENTS

Lord, I never knew that maturing meant I would have so many dumb moments. Many times, I say things that later I think were stupid. And I worry that everyone will think I'm pitiful. I remember hearing about Moses, who had trouble speaking in public and was nervous about doing what You asked, yet You were with him. So, I'm asking You to help me be the person You made me to be. I want to learn to be comfortable in a group and to be able to communicate well, but I don't want to constantly worry about what others think. I'm depending on You to help me get it right as I grow and learn. Amen.

My mouth will speak words of wisdom.
PSALM 49:3 NIV

Day 307
IT'S ABOUT TIME!

Lord, would You please help me manage my time better? I realize that to grow in You, I must spend time reading the scriptures and praying daily. But usually other worldly "things" distract me from the important matters of the heart. I confess that I spend too much time on activities that are unproductive. Your Word says there is a time for everything. I thank You that You have made enough hours in the day for me to accomplish everything I need to do, want to do, and should do. But I know it's about time that I give You time before anything or anyone else. Amen.

There is a time for everything.
ECCLESIASTES 3:1 NCV

Day 308
A BRAND-NEW HEART

God, I'm embarrassed by something I've done, and I come to You humbly, asking You to help me be a better person and not mess up so much. I know I'll never be perfect until I'm in heaven with You. . .but I really want to do the best I can for You right here. I'm ashamed by my actions. Please help me do the right thing! No matter what I do, You are always waiting for me with open arms and a heart overflowing with love. I love You, Lord. Thank You for wiping my slate clean and giving me a brand-new heart to start fresh again. Amen.

But you, Lord, are a compassionate and gracious
God, slow to anger, abounding in love and faithfulness.
PSALM 86:15 NIV

Day 309

GO AGAINST THE FLOW

I really want to be accepted by my friends, Jesus. Most of the time there isn't a problem—I'm not confronted with temptation too often. But You have told me not to go with the crowd if they're doing something wrong. That feels like walking against the current of a raging river sometimes. I can get swept away by peer pressure, or I can take a stand and act in a way pleasing to You. You don't promise that it will be an easy decision, but You do promise to be with me and to give me a way out. Lord Jesus, please give me the strength to choose what's right. In Your name, amen.

Don't copy the behavior and customs of this world, but let God transform you into a new person by changing the way you think. Then you will learn to know God's will for you, which is good and pleasing and perfect.
ROMANS 12:2 NLT

Day 310

A LITTLE RESPECT

Thank You, Lord, for the people You've placed in my life—parents, grandparents, aunts, uncles, teachers, leaders at my church. . .all of the wonderful people You've blessed me with. Show me how to give them respect, God. When I get frustrated with the authority figures in my life, please guard my tongue and help me to respond in a way that brings honor. May my actions reflect a respectful heart. And Lord, when I see other teens treating adults disrespectfully, give me the courage to let them know that what they're doing is wrong. Maybe I can set a good example by showing them how they should treat their elders. I'm going to try, for sure! Amen.

Never speak harshly to an older man, but appeal to him respectfully as you would to your own father. Talk to younger men as you would to your own brothers. Treat older women as you would your mother, and treat younger women with all purity as you would your own sisters.

1 Timothy 5:1–2 nlt

Day 311

WHEN IT'S HARD TO TRUST

Dear God, sometimes it's hard to trust because I've been hurt or let down by others in the past, and even though I know You are perfect and cannot let me down, I still find it hard to trust You with all my problems and doubts. There are so many examples of people in scripture who completely trusted You, like Esther when she married the king who was persecuting her people. If she could trust You in that situation, then I should be able to trust You with everything in my life. Thank You for Your patience with me, Lord, as I learn to trust You with everything in my life. Amen.

"God is the one who saves me; I will trust him and not be afraid. The LORD, the LORD gives me strength and makes me sing. He has saved me."

ISAIAH 12:2 NCV

Day 312

A GOOD NAME

I want to have a good reputation, Lord. When people think of me, I want them to think positive things. But a good reputation must be earned. It's the result of many wise decisions over a long period of time. A good reputation is the result of virtuous character. One important quality I need, if I want people to think well of me, is love. Another important quality is faithfulness. Help me to consistently live the qualities that will give me a good name, Lord. When people think of me, I want them to think of You. Amen.

Let love and faithfulness never leave you. . . . Then you will win favor and a good name in the sight of God and man.
PROVERBS 3:3–4 NIV

Day 313
LEVEL FAILED

Father, I keep making mistakes and don't know if I'll ever measure up. In the Bible, I find that there are many people who failed. Eve ate the fruit You told her not to, and then she convinced Adam to sin as well. Sarah laughed when You promised that she'd have a baby in her old age. . . . I see that even if I fail, good can come from it. I can be restored to a right relationship with You. Thank You for not expecting me to be perfect. You only ask that I obey and walk in Your way, and when I do fail, that I repent and move on, continuing to follow You. Amen.

My flesh and my heart may fail, but God is the strength of my heart and my portion forever.
PSALM 73:26 NIV

Day 314
THE SUNNY SIDE

Help me, Father God, to fill my mind with good thoughts, things that are beautiful, not ugly. Things I can cheer for, not cry about. That doesn't mean I will ignore all the bad stuff. It's just that I'm going to focus on what's *good* in this world—not on what's evil. I want to live in Your light, not the dark. So help me, Lord, to walk and stay on the sunny side of the street each and every day, to say prayers for those who need them, and to praise You for all Your wonders here on earth. Amen.

Fix your thoughts on what is true, and honorable, and right, and pure, and lovely, and admirable. Think about things that are excellent and worthy of praise. Keep putting into practice all you learned and received from me—everything you heard from me and saw me doing. Then the God of peace will be with you.
PHILIPPIANS 4:8–9 NLT

Day 315
CALM THE STORMS

Calm the storms in my heart, Lord Jesus. It seems my whole world is crashing down. Everything is changing. And yet, I feel so stuck at this in-between age. Lord, You know all about storms and struggles. You lived here in this world. You were betrayed by some of Your closest friends. You never even had a home to call Your own. You were arrested for no wrong-doing and then crucified. Thank You for coming to earth and living as a man. It helps me to know that You understand my heartache. Calm my storms, Lord, and if some of them must continue for now, just hold me. I feel safe with You, Jesus. Amen.

Jesus answered, "Why are you afraid? You don't have enough faith." Then Jesus got up and gave a command to the wind and the waves, and it became completely calm. The men were amazed and said, "What kind of man is this? Even the wind and the waves obey him!"
MATTHEW 8:26–27 NCV

Day 316
THE WORDS I SAY

God, it's so easy to pick up words that other people use—the good and the bad! I don't want to mimic others. I want to be like You! The best way to do that is to put into my heart and mind what is good and to choose words that are good. Jesus told His disciples that the words we speak come from our hearts (Matthew 15:18). That's where change starts. The things I think about, look at, the people I hang out with, whatever I focus on—that is what will show up in my speech. Help me focus on You, Your Word, and what pleases You, God. Amen.

The heart of the godly thinks carefully before speaking;
the mouth of the wicked overflows with evil words.
PROVERBS 15:28 NLT

Day 317
I WANT TO OBEY!

Thank You, Father, for my family. I love my parents, and I want to honor and obey them; but sometimes I don't. . .like when my mom tells me to empty the dishwasher, clean my room, finish my homework, or do something I'd rather not do at the moment. My parents often ask me to do things that are inconvenient or just poor timing. At least that's the way I feel. At those times, it's especially hard for me to obey. When obedience is hard, give me the strength to do what I know is right. I want to honor and respect You by honoring and showing my parents respect in all I say and do. Amen.

Children, obey your parents because you
belong to the Lord, for this is the right thing
to do. "Honor your father and mother."
EPHESIANS 6:1–2 NLT

Day 318
A FRAGILE JAR

Father, help me to remember who is in control of my life. I try to take control back from You sometimes, but then I'm reminded that I'm just a fragile jar that You have chosen to make Your home in. You are the source of the light in my heart. If others notice great things about me, give me the courage to tell them the story of You. Help me remember that You are the one who gives me power and strength. I want my life to be about Your love shining through me and not about me and what I can do on my own. Amen.

We now have this light shining in our hearts,
but we ourselves are like fragile clay jars containing
this great treasure. This makes it clear that our
great power is from God, not from ourselves.
2 CORINTHIANS 4:7 NLT

Day 319
CHOOSING FRIENDS

God, deep down, I know that if people don't like me unless I go against what I know is right, they're not really my friends. Those kinds of friends will only lead me into trouble. It's such a hard place to be, Lord. I don't want to be that weirdo in the corner who doesn't have any friends. I also don't want to behave badly just to be popular. Either way, I know I'll be unhappy. Help me choose my friends wisely, Lord. Send people into my life who will encourage me to make good decisions, who will encourage me to honor You. And help me to be that kind of friend to others as well. Amen.

The righteous choose their friends carefully,
but the way of the wicked leads them astray.
PROVERBS 12:26 NIV

Day 320
MEAN GIRLS

Ooh, some girls can be so mean, Lord! They act like they're better than everyone else. They play mean tricks on people. They lie and do other things that are just plain bad. Whenever I'm around girls who act like this, I want to be mean right back. But that's not what You ask me to do. It's not always easy to repay evil with good, but I'm going to give it my best shot, Father! The next time those mean girls start acting up, I'm going to turn the other cheek. It won't be easy, but maybe, if I really pray about it, I can win them over with Your love. Amen.

Don't repay evil for evil. Don't retaliate with insults when people insult you. Instead, pay them back with a blessing. That is what God has called you to do, and he will grant you his blessing.
1 Peter 3:9 nlt

Day 321
MY HOPE IS IN YOU

Dear Lord, I sometimes place my hope in places I shouldn't, like my friends, or my parents, or myself and my own abilities. Whenever I do this, I am always let down and disappointed by myself and others. Lord, please remind me that real hope and assurance come only from You. Teach me to look to You for everything I need and to expect great things from You. Even though it is so easy for me to get discouraged and forget to hope, I need Your reminders in my life. Amen.

In him our hearts rejoice, for we trust in his holy name. Let your unfailing love surround us, LORD, for our hope is in you alone.
PSALM 33:21–22 NLT

Day 322
A GREAT BIG "THANK YOU!"

Bad days? I know I will sometimes have them, Father—probably more often than I'd like. Even though I can't control the things that can and will go wrong, please help me to remember that I *can* control my reactions to those things. So, the next time I have a bad day, Father God, I'm asking for You to send me a little reminder of everything that's *wonderful* in my life: my family, my pet, my bedroom that's decorated just the way I like it, my very best friends. . .and most of all, *You!* I'm sending up a great big "thank You!" for everything good in my life. Amen.

Always give thanks for all things to God the Father in the name of our Lord Jesus Christ.
EPHESIANS 5:20 NLV

Day 323
SEEING ISN'T BELIEVING

Heavenly Father, I can't see You or touch You, but I have felt You in my soul, speaking to me. I have seen You working through my parents and my pastor and others. I have felt peace when I've prayed and forgiveness when I've asked for it. I have seen You answer prayers. So, I just want to say today that I believe in You even though I can't see You. I'm still maturing in my faith, but I know You're going to be there for me every day of my life. Thank You for sending Your Son to die for my sins so that I can have a relationship with You. In Jesus' name, amen.

Then Jesus told him, "You believe because you have seen me. Blessed are those who believe without seeing me."
JOHN 20:29 NLT

Day 324
BLESSINGS TO BLESS OTHERS

Lord, give me the energy to continue doing good things. Show me all the ways I can help or work with the people in my school, youth group, and church. Keep me from getting so busy with friends, sports, games, and activities that I don't have extra time to do things for others. Thank You for giving me the simple task, time, or talent to serve people in a way that shows them what You are all about and draws them closer to You. Keep energizing me as I use my blessings to bless others, starting with my family at home and church.

So let's not allow ourselves to get fatigued doing good. At the right time we will harvest a good crop if we don't give up, or quit. Right now, therefore, every time we get the chance, let us work for the benefit of all, starting with the people closest to us in the community of faith.

GALATIANS 6:9 MSG

EVERYTHING I NEED

You want to bless Your children, Father. I see a glimpse of this type of love when I look at earthly parents who give their kids good "stuff." Just as generous, caring moms and dads give their children food, clothing, and shelter, You provide this and so much more for Your children. You provide Christian friends for me to enjoy time with and grow alongside. You have provided a school and a church for me. My home and family are direct gifts from Your hands. You have given me everything I have—even my abilities and talents. Every good and perfect gift truly comes from You, my heavenly Father. I am so thankful. Amen.

And my God will supply all your needs according to His riches in glory in Christ Jesus. Now to our God and Father be the glory forever and ever. Amen.
PHILIPPIANS 4:19–20 NASB

Day 326

LOVE YOUR ENEMIES

I know You faced bullies, Jesus—those who crucified You were not only cruel, they enjoyed hurting You. Sometimes I think people like to see others suffer. I want to respond the way You did—with love—but I need Your help. It is not always easy to look on others with compassion and understanding. Please help me to see others as You do—to understand that often those who hurt us are in pain themselves. Thank You that when others were unkind to You, You loved them in spite of themselves, just as You love me! Amen.

"Love those who hate you. Do good to them. Let them use your things and do not expect something back. Your reward will be much. You will be the children of the Most High. He is kind to those who are not thankful and to those who are full of sin."

Luke 6:35 NLV

Day 327
NEVER ALONE

Sometimes I feel alone, even with family and friends around me. I don't get it. At those times, Father, remind me that You are always with me—that I'm never alone. Before I even speak one word in prayer, You are there. You understand how I feel and why I feel that way. Thank You for being so close and caring so much. You promised to never leave or reject me no matter what. So help me to remember that even when I feel alone, I'm not. You're at my side at all times. Amen.

Where could I go to escape from your Spirit or from your sight? If I were to climb up to the highest heavens, you would be there. If I were to dig down to the world of the dead you would also be there. Suppose I had wings like the dawning day and flew across the ocean. Even then your powerful arm would guide and protect me.
PSALM 139:7–10 CEV

Day 328

SHINING THROUGH

Lord Jesus, remind me that no matter how fat or skinny, small or tall, fashionable or unfashionable I feel, that's not what's important. As long as I'm neat and clean, You are happy with how I look on the outside, whether I'm in old jeans and a T-shirt with my hair in a messy bun or wearing a new outfit and the latest hairstyle. Instead, Your concern is that I am beautiful on the *inside*. Lord, help me to spend more time on my inner rather than outer beauty—for my inner beauty will glow forever. Thank You for loving me for what is within my heart. Amen.

Don't depend on things like fancy hairdos or gold jewelry or expensive clothes to make you look beautiful. Be beautiful in your heart by being gentle and quiet. This kind of beauty will last, and God considers it very special.
1 PETER 3:3–4 CEV

Day 329
GOT ATTITUDE?

It isn't fair when I have to clean up someone else's mess, Lord! And it's infuriating when I get blamed for something I didn't do. I try to defend myself (and sometimes say a bit more than that!) so that the world knows I'm innocent and mad that I was blamed. But that reaction isn't the right one, Father. You didn't defend Yourself when You had every right to do so. I want to learn from Your example. The next time I'm accused of something I didn't do, please remind me to breathe and count to ten. I also ask for grace to do what I'm asked anyway, even if it wasn't a result of anything I did. I need Your strength, Lord. Amen.

Do all things without grumbling or disputing, that you may be blameless and innocent, children of God without blemish in the midst of a crooked and twisted generation, among whom you shine as lights in the world.
PHILIPPIANS 2:14–15 ESV

Day 330

TAKING TIME TO TALK

Spending time with You is a privilege, God. The Bible says that You listen when I talk to You. You take me seriously. And I can ask You tough questions. Nothing's too hard for You, Lord! If I ask You to heal my grandmother's backache, You can do it! If I ask You to protect my dad while he's on his way to work, You can do that too. You're definitely the most powerful friend I've ever had. Just one more reason why I love hanging out with You. I'm always amazed by You! Amen.

And we are confident that he hears us whenever
we ask for anything that pleases him. And since we
know he hears us when we make our requests,
we also know that he will give us what we ask for.
1 John 5:14–15 nlt

Day 331
SECURITY IN GOD

Lord, I get so afraid sometimes. I worry about things that I have no control over. Whenever I start to worry, I need to remember that You are in control and will keep me safe. Remind me to tell You all my fears and give them over to You, for only You can comfort me during those times. Thank You for all the times that You remind me of Your love and protection and help me to trust You with every worry and fear that I have. Help me in the future when I struggle with fear and insecurity. Amen.

You need not be afraid of sudden disaster or the destruction that comes upon the wicked, for the LORD is your security. He will keep your foot from being caught in a trap.
PROVERBS 3:25–26 NLT

Day 332
JUST A TEENAGER

I'm just a teenager, Lord. And some people may look down on me because of my young age, Lord, but I know You don't. I know You've put me here for a reason and that purpose doesn't begin later. My purpose doesn't start when I graduate or when I get a job or get married or have children. My purpose here on earth began the day I was born. Before that, even. Lord, help me to live out Your purpose for me every single day, starting today. Amen.

Don't let anyone look down on you because you are young, but set an example for the believers in speech, in conduct, in love, in faith and in purity.
1 Timothy 4:12 niv

Day 333
HAVE PATIENCE

God, You said patience is a good thing. You also said it's important to be happy despite whatever is going on in our lives. Not that we must like everything, but You want us to keep trusting You and not freak out about stuff. It's called "being content." It's funny, Lord. I want people to be patient with me, but I'm not always patient with others. I want the people in my life to be calm and gentle no matter the circumstance, but I don't always act that way myself. Help me to have patience and be content, no matter what happens in my life today. Amen.

For I have learned to be content whatever the circumstances.
PHILIPPIANS 4:11 NIV

Day 334
STRENGTH IN ALL THINGS

When I forget to include You in my day, Father God, I end up feeling tired, uncertain, and sometimes a bit frightened. So help me to remember to take strength from You and arm myself with Your Word before I start each new day—I know that I can be ready for anyone and anything when I am staying close to You. Right now I am going to take time to rest in Your gentle care, Lord, knowing that You will give me the spiritual, mental, and physical muscle to do all I need to do. Focused on You, I can do all that You have created me to do. Amen.

I have strength for all things in Christ Who empowers me [I am ready for anything and equal to anything through Him Who infuses inner strength into me].
PHILIPPIANS 4:13 AMPC

Day 335

SECURITY IN THE LORD

Heavenly Father, I don't mean to worry. It's a bad habit. I don't want to be a worrier now or in the future when I'm an adult. Your Word tells me not to worry about tomorrow because every day has enough concerns of its own. I know I don't need to look into an unknown future with fear. Take the burden of my worries, Lord. I lay my concerns at Your feet. In You and You alone, I find security. Give me strength to face each day as it comes, and remind me that You've got my back! Thank You, God. Amen.

And when I was burdened with worries,
you comforted me and made me feel secure.
PSALM 94:19 CEV

Day 336
CAN YOU HEAR ME NOW, GOD?

God, the truth is, even though I *feel* like You aren't there—You are! I remember that Jesus said, "I will never leave you; I will never abandon you" (Hebrews 13:5 NCV). That means that on those days when I feel as if my prayers don't rise higher than the ceiling, You *are* still there. You care about my problems; You are listening and ready to help me. You are working in my life. Lord, I can't understand all the reasons why sometimes it seems like You are slow to act, but I want to learn to trust You. To believe that You love me and care about what happens in my life. Thank You. Amen.

"Be sure of this: I am with you always,
even to the end of the age."
MATTHEW 28:20 NLT

Day 337

TRUE FRIENDSHIP

What does true friendship look like? Loyalty and honesty are important to relationships. Real friends talk about more than just surface level things. They keep confidences and don't tell others your secrets. A true friend is someone you can trust. Am I that kind of friend to others, God? Can they count on me to be there for them, to care about their circumstances of life? In order to have a friend, I know I must be a friend. Help me be a true friend, God. One who loves no matter what. Help me be loyal and honest and think about others before myself. Amen.

Dear friends, let us continue to love one another, for love comes from God. Anyone who loves is a child of God and knows God.
1 JOHN 4:7 NLT

Day 338
GOD IS FAITHFUL

Father, I'm making Psalm 89 my prayer today: "I will sing of the LORD's unfailing love forever! Young and old will hear of your faithfulness. Your unfailing love will last forever. Your faithfulness is as enduring as the heavens. . . . All heaven will praise your great wonders. . . . For who in all of heaven can compare with the LORD? What mightiest angel is anything like the LORD? . . . He is far more awesome than all who surround his throne. O LORD God of Heaven's Armies! Where is there anyone as mighty as you, O LORD? You are entirely faithful" (Psalm 89:1–2, 5–8 NLT). Thank You, heavenly Father! Amen.

But the Lord is faithful; he will strengthen you and guard you from the evil one. . . . May the Lord lead your hearts into a full understanding and expression of the love of God and the patient endurance that comes from Christ.
2 THESSALONIANS 3:3, 5 NLT

Day 339
THAT'S WHAT I THINK

Dear Father, thank You for not condemning me for the thoughts I think. You know all about me—the horrible thoughts I have—and yet You still forgive me and love me. I want to train my mind so I can think of things that are of You—things that are good and pure. I can refuse to compromise on what I watch and read. I can choose friends who will speak in an acceptable way. I can talk kindly to my family (that one can be the hardest!). But all those decisions take some mental preparation. Fill my mind with Your love and goodness so that my thoughts reflect Your ways. In Your name, amen.

So letting your sinful nature control your mind leads to death.
But letting the Spirit control your mind leads to life and peace.
ROMANS 8:6 NLT

Day 340
CHOICES, CHOICES!

Wow, there are a lot of choices to make in life! I want to make the right ones every time, but it's so overwhelming sometimes. I get confused and don't know what to do. Can You help me make better choices, Father? Help me choose better things to watch on TV, better ways to respond when people hurt my feelings, and better foods that are healthier for my body. Help me to choose love over hate, joy over anger, and peace over arguing. I need Your help, Lord! Whenever I start to make a bad choice, whisper the words *"Make a better choice!"* in my ear. Amen.

"Watch and pray so that you will not fall into temptation.
The spirit is willing, but the flesh is weak."
MATTHEW 26:41 NIV

Day 341
YOUR CREATION

Dear Lord, I am so grateful for the beautiful world You created. For the blue sky, the rainy days, the green hills, and the sandy beaches. I'm thankful for the vast variety of animals that You created, from the cute puppy to the terrifying hammerhead shark; they were all designed by You! And each creation is a reminder of the care that You take when You create. If I ever doubt Your presence, all I need to do is look outside and be reminded of Your care. When I'm feeling small and insignificant, remind me of how You provide for the birds of the air and how much more You provide for me. Amen.

"And to all the beasts of the earth and all the birds in the sky and all the creatures that move along the ground—everything that has the breath of life in it— I give every green plant for food." And it was so.
GENESIS 1:30 NIV

Day 342
STAYING CLOSE

I don't know what to say to sad people, Lord. I often end up saying too much or saying something that makes it worse. I've tried giving gifts and doing things for them, but no matter what I do, I usually can't fix the problem. I guess the best thing I can do is just be there. Just stay close and let them know I care. You said You are close to the brokenhearted, Lord. Maybe that's what I should do too. Just stay close. Help me to know how to comfort hurting people, Lord. Give me wisdom to know when to speak and when to remain quiet, when to act and when to just stay close. Amen.

The LORD is close to the brokenhearted and
saves those who are crushed in spirit.
PSALM 34:18 NIV

Day 343

UNDER MY SKIN

Dear God, I've been thinking about my moods. Sometimes I feel cool and confident, and then other times I am so uptight. I wish I could stay calm all the time, but I can't. I'm asking You now, God, to help me deal with these moods. You can give me the strength to act nicely even when I feel yucky or when things are going wrong all day. I try to dress myself nicely, but I'm asking You today to help me dress my spirit well too. I want what's under my skin, the real me, to be attractive. Please help me think about what I do and say so that the beauty of Jesus will be seen in me. Amen.

Let everything you say be good and helpful, so that your words will be an encouragement to those who hear them.
EPHESIANS 4:29 NLT

Day 344

A DAUGHTER'S FAITH

Lord, I love the Bible story about the woman who had been bleeding for many years and had seen many doctors. When she heard about Your Son, she had one goal—to touch Him. She knew in her heart that Jesus could heal her. Then Jesus, knowing His power had gone out from Him, looked around to see who had touched Him. When the woman confessed that she had done it, Jesus had amazing words for her: "Daughter, your faith has healed you" (Mark 5:34 NIV). May those words be the ones I take right into my heart. May the idea that at any time I can reach out, touch You, and be better, be planted firmly in my mind. Amen.

When she heard about Jesus, she came up behind him in the crowd and touched his cloak, because she thought, "If I just touch his clothes, I will be healed." Immediately her bleeding stopped and she felt in her body that she was freed from her suffering.
MARK 5:27–29 NIV

Day 345
LULLABY FROM GOD

I find it amazing, God, that Your Word says You "rejoice over me with singing." The God of the universe taking time out of His busy schedule to sing a lullaby over me. . . now that is an awesome thought! Father, thank You for loving me the way you do—without condition, regardless of the circumstances, and even when I am not as faithful as I should be. You are sovereign and all-knowing. You are a Mighty Warrior who saves Your children. You created me, and You are delighted with me as Your daughter. You even sing over me in joy. I must be pretty special to You, Lord. I am so blessed. Amen.

"The Lord your God is with you, the Mighty Warrior who saves. He will take great delight in you; in his love he will no longer rebuke you, but will rejoice over you with singing."
ZEPHANIAH 3:17 NIV

Day 346
LOVING OTHERS

I like hanging around people who encourage me. It's easy to get focused on just my friends and forget to include others. What if my friends don't accept others into our group? Or what if I reach out to someone, and they reject my offer of friendship? It's hard to move beyond my own circle of close friends and look for those who may need encouragement themselves. Give me courage to act kindly and reach out and love others, God. Help me to be a friend to someone who might not have many friends or needs some encouragement of their own today. Amen.

Don't just pretend to love others. Really love them. Hate what is wrong. Hold tightly to what is good. Love each other with genuine affection, and take delight in honoring each other.
ROMANS 12:9–10 NLT

Day 347
I'M READY FOR CHANGE!

Change is difficult, Lord. I don't like or understand some of the changes in my life. Habits are hard to change too because I'm so used to doing the same things. I like to watch my favorite shows, and I enjoy texting with friends. If I can't do those things, it bothers me. I know that change is a part of life, and I need to adjust. But how? Only You can help me, Father. Your Word tells me that some changes are good for me, and I shouldn't resist them. Help me to make the changes in my life that will bring inner growth. Amen.

And our faces are not covered. We all show the Lord's glory, and we are being changed to be like him. This change in us brings more and more glory, which comes from the Lord.
2 CORINTHIANS 3:18 ERV

AMBASSADORS FOR GOD

God, I've learned that reconciliation means making things right with someone. You've done that with the whole world through Jesus. You sent Your Son to bear all of our sins on His body on the cross so that we might die to sins and live for You (1 Peter 2:24). But we still must do our part, Lord—to accept Your gift and allow Christ to make His home in our hearts. Now that I understand that, I know You've given me the job of sharing You with others. I'm Your ambassador—Your representative. That is a great responsibility that I don't take lightly, Lord. Help me to share with others boldly and in a way that shows love and light. Amen.

For God was in Christ, reconciling the world to himself, no longer counting people's sins against them. And he gave us this wonderful message of reconciliation. So we are Christ's ambassadors. . . . We speak for Christ when we plead, "Come back to God!"
2 CORINTHIANS 5:19–20 NLT

Day 349
HEALTHY HABITS

My request today, Father, is that You will help me to find balance in my life. I want to be healthy—and I want to take care of myself. And I know that You want me to be healthy too; and yet You don't ask me to always deprive myself to please You. Help me know how to do this right, please. And help me remember to feed my soul with healthy food Your Word—the best way to live a happy, healthy life! Amen.

How sweet are your words to my taste,
sweeter than honey to my mouth!
PSALM 119:103 NIV

Day 350
DON'T BE A BUSYBODY!

Heavenly Father, help me to remember that people have boundaries. They need their own space, just like I need mine! I'm not supposed to get in their business unless they ask me to, and even then I just need to pray for them, not try to fix their problems. And Lord, when people get in my business—when the busybodies in my life try to weasel their way into my problems and situations—help me to respond graciously. I want to be kind and loving, even when nosy people try to fix my problems. Here's my new motto, Father: "Say no to nosiness!" With Your help, I can do it! Amen.

For we hear that some among you are leading an undisciplined life, doing no work at all, but acting like busybodies.
2 THESSALONIANS 3:11 NASB

Day 351
FORGIVING OTHERS

Heavenly Father, help me to forgive my friends and family when they hurt me. It is so hard to forgive someone when I am hurting and upset or when I feel rejected and alone. Sometimes I would rather just walk away and never forgive the person I am angry at, but I know that is not what You would want me to do. Soften my heart to them and help me to forgive them just as You have forgiven me and everyone else in the world. Help me to look to Your example when I don't want to forgive someone and remember how many times You have forgiven me. Thank You for Your never-ending patience with me. Amen.

"If you forgive those who sin against you, your heavenly Father will forgive you. But if you refuse to forgive others, your Father will not forgive your sins."
MATTHEW 6:14–15 NLT

Day 352
GETTING EVEN

When people are mean, Lord, I want to be meaner. I want to plot and plan and get even and show them they'd better not mess with me again. But I know that's not Your way, Lord. When I react in anger, the other person will just react in a bigger, uglier way, and then it will be my turn to outdo them, and the drama will grow. Instead, I need to do the right, good, kind, loving, caring thing, even when those around me don't. Lord, give me wisdom, and help me do what's right even when I am hurt. I want others to see what a difference You make in our lives. Amen.

Do not repay anyone evil for evil. Be careful to do what is right in the eyes of everyone.
ROMANS 12:17 NIV

Day 353
MORE THAN BACKGROUND

I'm wanting to listen to more music, God, but I think I need Your opinion first. It's easy just to choose whatever my friends like; still, I don't think that's the best way. Some people say it doesn't really matter, that the words aren't really that important. But I know that, for me, music is more than background noise. I want to honor You with the music I listen to because I know it affects my attitude and my relationship with You. Please help me make good choices in the music I stream and download and listen to. I want You to be Lord over this area of my life too. In Jesus' name, amen.

---

*And whatever you do, whether in word or deed,
do it all in the name of the Lord Jesus, giving
thanks to God the Father through him.*
COLOSSIANS 3:17 NIV

ASK, SEEK, KNOCK

Lord, Your Word promises that Your plans for me are good. And I believe You! I really do want to follow You with all my heart. Please keep my eyes and ears from evil and firmly set Your Word in my heart. Thank You for the Holy Spirit living inside my heart, who guides me and reminds me of everything I need to know each day. I'm Yours, Lord. Help me seek after You all the days of my life and not worry so much about the future. You've got this, God. And I trust Your faithfulness!

"Ask, and it will be given to you; seek, and you will find; knock, and it will be opened to you. For everyone who asks receives, and the one who seeks finds, and to the one who knocks it will be opened."

MATTHEW 7:7–8 ESV

Day 355
THE LOVE OF MONEY

Help me, Lord, to be happy with the things I already have and not be constantly working toward acquiring that "next thing." I know I am so blessed and that many people do not even have necessities such as food and water. Give me eyes to see beyond the glitter and glamour of the things of my world to the hurt of theirs. Help me to use my resources to help others. You are what lasts, God. You will never leave me. I want You more than I want the things of this world. Amen.

Don't fall in love with money. Be satisfied with what you have.
The Lord has promised that he will not leave us or desert us.
HEBREWS 13:5 CEV

Day 356
STARTING OVER

God, the apostle Paul talks about his struggle with sin and doing what's right in Romans 7. I'm like him—I want to do what's right, but I don't always succeed. When I don't get it right, I need to start over. The first step is coming to You, God, and telling You all about it. You understand and forgive. To me that is amazing, especially when I find myself doing the same wrong thing over and over again. Confessing is just agreeing that You are right, that Your way is the best, the only way. Help me when I fail to turn to You. Thank You for forgiving me and giving me another chance. Amen.

If we claim that we're free of sin, we're only fooling ourselves. A claim like that is errant nonsense. On the other hand, if we admit our sins—simply come clean about them—he won't let us down; he'll be true to himself. He'll forgive our sins and purge us of all wrongdoing.
1 JOHN 1:8–9 MSG

MORE ABOUT YOU, LESS ABOUT ME!

Lord, sometimes I think more about myself than I think about You. I don't mean to; it just happens. My mind fills up with things, and I get wrapped up in my own thoughts. I know it's selfish to think too much about myself. I'm glad You're not like that. You are unselfish, loving, and considerate. I want to be like You, Father. The Bible says that You are always thinking about me. That is so awesome and incredible. I want to think of You the same way. When too many of my thoughts are about me, help me to become Christlike and redirect my thoughts more toward You and others. Amen.

How precious to me are your thoughts, God! How vast is the sum of them! Were I to count them, they would outnumber the grains of sand—when I awake, I am still with you.
PSALM 139:17–18 NIV

Day 358
FRIENDSHIPS THAT HONOR GOD

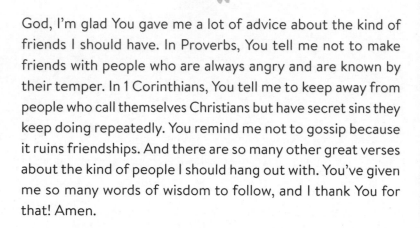

God, I'm glad You gave me a lot of advice about the kind of friends I should have. In Proverbs, You tell me not to make friends with people who are always angry and are known by their temper. In 1 Corinthians, You tell me to keep away from people who call themselves Christians but have secret sins they keep doing repeatedly. You remind me not to gossip because it ruins friendships. And there are so many other great verses about the kind of people I should hang out with. You've given me so many words of wisdom to follow, and I thank You for that! Amen.

Don't befriend angry people or associate with
hot-tempered people, or you will learn to be
like them and endanger your soul.
PROVERBS 22:24–25 NLT

Day 359
RENEW MY STRENGTH

I'm tired, Lord. I know I'm young, but life is hard! I'm thankful that my hope is in You, heavenly Father. I can come to You and spend time with You. I can find refreshment for my weary soul when I pray and read Your Word. My strength is renewed when I just rest in You and let You have the worries of my day. Thank You for giving me the endurance that I need to live life one day at a time. I love You! Amen.

The Lord God is my strength. He has made my feet like the feet of a deer, and He makes me walk on high places.
HABAKKUK 3:19 NLV

Day 360
STAYING ACTIVE
IN CHURCH

God, I love being part of my church. It's the perfect place to mature in You. Talk about great people! I'm surrounded on every side. Help me to find a way to fit in so that my gifts can be used. I want to worship with my friends and family, but I also want You to use me to reach other people. I love my church friends—old and new—and I love the adults too. It's a great place to hang out. Best of all, Lord, it's an amazing place to worship You! When I go to church, I can stand with other Christians and sing songs of praise. That makes me the happiest of all. Amen.

You should not stay away from the church meetings, as some are doing, but you should meet together and encourage each other. Do this even more as you see the day coming.
HEBREWS 10:25 NCV

Day 361
INNER BEAUTY

Heavenly Father, when I really think about it, the thing that draws me to others isn't the way they look or how they dress. The thing that makes me want to spend time with someone is their personality. How do they treat me? How do they make me feel about myself when I'm around them? I guess that's what you call inner beauty. And if it's what draws me to other people, I'll bet that's what will draw others to me. Lord, help me to spend more time on my inner beauty—on making others feel loved, accepted, and important than on what I look like on the outside. Amen.

Let your adorning be the hidden person of the heart with the imperishable beauty of a gentle and quiet spirit.
1 PETER 3:4 ESV

Day 362
MY PARENTS

I want to make my parents proud of me, Lord. But sometimes it's hard. . .like when they don't see things the way I see them, or they don't let me do the things I want to do. My parents may not be perfect, but they love me more than anyone else in this world, besides You, God. They want what's best for me. So, help me to honor them with the way I treat them in person and the way I act when they're not around. I want them to know they can trust me. I want them to know I'll do the right thing, out of respect for them. In everything I do, I want to bring joy to their hearts—and to Yours. Amen.

A wise son brings joy to his father, but a foolish son brings grief to his mother.

PROVERBS 10:1 NIV

Day 363

ALL THINGS WORK TOGETHER FOR GOOD

Lord, sometimes I just don't understand. Your Word says that all things work together for good. But this doesn't feel good. It feels *awful*. It seems like everything goes wrong for me. I know that I have many blessings, but I just don't understand why You let certain things happen. The Bible tells me to cast my cares on You because You care for me. I lay them at Your feet, God. Help me not to scramble to pick up my worries again but to leave them with You. You are big enough to handle all my hurts, disappointments, and confusion. Work all things together in my life, Father. Work them together for good. . . even when I don't understand. Amen.

And we know that in all things God works for the good of those who love him, who have been called according to his purpose.

ROMANS 8:28 NIV

Day 364

HELLO? IS ANYONE THERE?

God, sometimes I get so busy that I forget to spend time with You, and that's not good. I don't want You to have to come looking for me. I don't want You to have to say, *"Hello? Is anyone there?..."* There's a lot of stuff on my calendar. I'm a busy girl! But there's nothing else I can possibly do that will be more important than spending time with You, my God. The Bible is my personal invitation to spend time with You. Draw me close to You. May I never forget You, even on my busiest day! Amen.

Don't let the excitement of youth cause you to forget your Creator. Honor him in your youth before you grow old and say, "Life is not pleasant anymore."
ECCLESIASTES 12:1 NLT

Day 365

MY BEDTIME PRAYER

Dear Father, once again, You have faithfully brought me through another day. You have met my needs—food, clothing, and shelter—and have blessed me beyond that. I spent time with those I love. You kept me safe and have given me a place to sleep. I can lie down, confident that You will be watching me all night long because You never sleep. Nothing can happen to me that You do not allow. Tomorrow, may I wake full of Your joy and face the day with a positive attitude. May I be a blessing to each person I encounter. And may I grow even closer to You as I continue my journey. Good night! Amen.

In peace I will lie down and sleep, for you alone, LORD, make me dwell in safety.

PSALM 4:8 NIV

CONTRIBUTOR INDEX

Emily Biggers is a Tennessee native living in Arlington, Texas. She loves to travel, write, spend time with family and friends, and decorate.

Renae Brumbaugh is a freelance writer, author, syndicated newspaper columnist, teacher, and mom. In her free time, she leaps tall buildings in a single bound and rescues kittens out of trees. Or at least she might try to do those things if she had free time. . . .

Jennifer Hahn is a freelance writer, editor, and proofreader. She lives in Pennsylvania's Amish country with her husband and three children.

Janice Thompson hails from south Texas. She is a Christian author and mother of four grown daughters.

Janice's Readings: 20, 40, 42, 50, 51, 70, 71, 80, 90, 100, 108, 110, 120, 140, 150, 160, 170, 180, 190, 200, 210, 220, 230, 240, 250, 260, 268, 280, 290, 310, 320, 330, 340, 350, 360, 364

Missy Horsfall, a pastor's wife for more than twenty years, is a Bible study teacher, board member, and speaker for Circle of Friends Ministries.

Missy's Readings: Days 6, 16, 26, 36, 56, 66, 76, 85, 86, 94, 96, 103, 106, 126, 136, 146, 156, 158, 166, 186, 196, 226, 236, 246, 256, 266, 286, 293, 296, 316, 326, 336, 337, 346, 356

Tina Krause is a freelance writer, editor, and award-winning newspaper columnist in Valparaiso, Indiana. She and her husband, Jim, have five grandchildren.

Tina's Readings: Days 17, 27, 37, 47, 57, 62, 67, 77, 87, 97, 101, 107, 117, 118, 127, 137, 147, 167, 177, 187, 197, 207, 217, 227, 237, 247, 257, 267, 283, 287, 297, 307, 317, 327, 347, 357

Donna Maltese is a freelance writer, editor, and proofreader as well as a pastor's prayer partner. She lives in Pennsylvania with her family.

Donna's Readings: 4, 8, 14, 34, 46, 74, 84, 91, 98, 104, 124, 125, 144, 154, 164, 174, 184, 194, 201, 204, 214, 222, 234, 235, 244, 245, 254, 270, 284, 294, 303, 304, 314, 324, 328, 334, 344

Prayers by Donna Maltese were inspired by the following girls, ages 10 to 14, from three different families—Kendall, Madalynne, and Hannah Geib; Grace and Lizzie Hogue; Sydni and Savannah Stockert.

Kelly McIntosh serves as vice president of editorial at a Christian publishing house. She and her husband, John, live in Ohio with their twin son and daughter.

Kelly's Readings: Days 143, 223, 322

Brigitta Nortker takes every opportunity to travel that she can. In her free time she enjoys an excellent book, a cup of coffee, and spending time with friends and family.

Brigitta's Readings: Days 1, 10, 11, 21, 30, 31, 41, 44, 52, 60, 61, 81, 111, 121, 131, 134, 151, 157, 161, 171, 181, 191, 192, 211, 221, 231, 241, 251, 261, 271, 291, 301, 311, 321, 331, 341, 351

MariLee Parrish lives in Colorado with her husband, Eric, and young children. She's a freelance musician and writer who desires to paint a picture of God with her life, talents, and ministries.

MariLee's Readings: Days 7, 18, 24, 28, 38, 48, 49, 58, 78, 114, 116, 128, 130, 138, 168, 178, 188, 198, 208, 218, 228, 238, 248, 258, 275, 276, 278, 288, 298, 300, 308, 318, 338, 348, 354, 358

Valorie Quesenberry is a pastor's wife, mother, musician, editor of a Christian ladies' magazine, and writer. She periodically contributes devotionals to a Christian literature provider.

Valorie's Readings: Days 3, 13, 15, 22, 23, 43, 63, 64, 73, 83, 93, 123, 142, 153, 163, 173, 176, 183, 193, 213, 232, 233, 243, 253, 263, 273, 306, 323, 343, 349, 353

SCRIPTURE INDEX
OLD TESTAMENT

NEW TESTAMENT

MORE ENCOURAGEMENT FOR YOUR BEAUTIFUL SPIRIT!

You Belong
Devotions and Prayers for a Teen Girl's Heart

*You Were Created with Purpose by a Loving, Heavenly Creator
. . .You Belong!*

This delightful devotional is a lovely reminder of that you were created with purpose by a heavenly Creator. . .and that you belong—right here and now—in this world. 180 encouraging readings and inspiring prayers, rooted in biblical truth, will reassure your uncertain heart, helping you to understand that you're never alone and always loved. In each devotional reading, you will encounter the bountiful blessings and grace of your Creator, while coming to trust His purposeful plan for you in this world.

Flexible Casebound / 978-1-63609-169-3